AMERICAN ORIENTAL SERIES
VOLUME 51

ALEXANDER HAMILTON
(1762-1824)

A CHAPTER IN THE EARLY HISTORY OF SANSKRIT PHILOLOGY

AMERICAN ORIENTAL SERIES

VOLUME 51

AMERICAN ORIENTAL SOCIETY
NEW HAVEN, CONNECTICUT

1968

ALEXANDER HAMILTON
(1762-1824)

A CHAPTER IN THE EARLY HISTORY OF SANSKRIT PHILOLOGY

BY

ROSANE ROCHER

Research Fellow
National Foundation for Scientific Research (Belgium)

AMERICAN ORIENTAL SOCIETY
NEW HAVEN, CONNECTICUT

1968

Made in the United States of America

J. H. FURST COMPANY, BALTIMORE, MARYLAND

PREFACE

Some books are written by accident. During the Fall Term of 1965 we availed ourselves of a prolonged stay in England to become a daily visitor to the British Museum Library. The idea was to collect additional materials for an article dealing with the reactions toward Pāṇini in the West, on which we had been working intermittently for a number of years. The first period envisaged by the article was to concentrate upon the first Western scholars who had learned Sanskrit from pandits. It contained an incidental reference to a Sanskritist named Alexander Hamilton. In the course of our attempts to learn more about that scholar than the few sentences by Windisch provide, we were struck by certain inconsistencies in the various general sources we consulted. We pursued our researches, and what we found induced us to persevere: this man about whom so little was known revealed himself as a scholar of no little importance in the history of Sanskrit studies and comparative philology,—and an attractive personality as well.

The major portion of the research was carried out in London, during the last trimester of 1965, and during two other brief visits in March and July 1966. We gladly acknowledge the help we enjoyed there from various persons and institutions. The British Museum Library is the scholar's paradise. Along with the wonderful collections which are kept—and well catalogued—there, we highly appreciated the amability of the attendants at the various reading rooms. Moreover, as on many previous occasions, we could count on the friendliness of Mr. W. Zwalf, of the Department of Oriental Books and Manuscripts; his initiative and enthusiasm were of great help to us. At the India Office Library we obtained every support, as always, from Mr. S. C. Sutton and his staff. We should mention in particular the effective help we enjoyed from Mr. M. Muir, who introduced us to the records of the East India Company, unknown to us previously. Mr. J. D. Pearson, the librarian of the School of Oriental and African Studies in the University of London, kindly allowed us to borrow several important books. We were also received most cordially at the Public Record Office, where we were granted permission to publish the only autograph letter by Hamilton known so far. Our very warm thanks also go to Mr. I. Kaye, the librarian of the Royal Society, who allowed us to consult and publish the election certificate of Hamilton, and who, after our return to Belgium, was kind enough to send us a Xerox copy of that document, as well as provide the identification of the signatures thereon.

The Times Literary Supplement accorded us space in its columns to launch an appeal for information about unpublished documents concerning Hamilton. Our hearty thanks go to the two scholars who reacted to that appeal. Dr. H. C. Aarsleff, of Princeton University, gave us useful data with regard to Friedrich

Schlegel especially. Mr. P. M. Rosenberg, of Oxford, drew our attention to the above mentioned autograph letter which is preserved at the Public Record Office.

After our return to Belgium we used the facilities of the library of the University of Brussels, and worked at the Belgian Royal Library, which also made it possible to obtain a number of books through interlibrary loan.

In Paris, we were allowed to consult Hamilton's autograph catalogue of Sanskrit manuscripts in the National Library, as well as other manuscript documents of great importance for our researches; we also obtained permission to publish extracts from them. Our special thanks also go to the staff of the French National Archives, who gave us all possible help during the week we spent with them.

Several scholars have most graciously replied to our requests for specific information. We should mention Prof. Dr. F. Bäthgen, the historian of the Munich Academy, who gave us full details about Hamilton's election to that institution; Dr. J. Gaulmier, Professor in the University of Strasbourg and Volney's biographer, who communicated useful data with regard to Volney; and Mrs. Dr. U. Struc-Oppenberg, who provided us with additional information about Friedrich Schlegel's Sanskrit studies.

Shortly after our arrival in the United States we handed over the manuscript of this book to Dr. W. Norman Brown, emeritus Professor of Sanskrit in the University of Pennsylvania. May this be an opportunity to thank him not only for his suggestions which made the text more lucid, but also for his continuous and overwhelming kindness which meant so much for one newly arrived in this country.

Very useful also were a number of remarks made in the margin of the manuscript by Dr. Holden Furber.

The text was then submitted to Dr. Ernest Bender. We are most grateful to him, not only because he consented to read the manuscript and propose a number of valuable emendations, but also because he presented it to the American Oriental Society for publication.

Finally, may we be permitted to acknowledge the help we received from our husband. All problems on which we felt there might be any discussion were submitted to him first. We can only hope that Alexander Hamilton's biography will be judged interesting enough to justify the time he devoted to it.

Philadelphia, October 5, 1966.

POSTSCRIPT

After this work was completed, the *Wellesley Index to Victorian Periodicals* (vol. 1) was published by the University of Toronto Press. The *Index* attempts to identify the contributors to various journals among which the *Edinburgh Review.* The identifications are based mainly on unpublished materials: correspondence between and memoirs of editors and contributors to the journal. It was a great pleasure for us to see that the articles which we attributed to Hamilton on the basis of purely internal criteria almost uniformly correspond to those ascribed to him in the *Index.* Although we could not make adequate use of the *Index* in the text of this volume, we were able to incorporate into the notes the evidence adduced by the *Wellesley Index to Victorian Periodicals* (abbreviated *WIVP*).

Philadelphia, July 10, 1967.

TABLE OF CONTENTS

PREFACE vii

TABLE OF CONTENTS xi

INTRODUCTION 1

CHAPTER I. THE EARLY YEARS 3

CHAPTER II. CALCUTTA: THE DISCOVERY OF SANSKRIT 5
- The Bengal Army 5
- The Discovery of Sanskrit 5
- Resignation from the Army 8

CHAPTER III. GREAT BRITAIN: THE FIRST PUBLICATIONS 11
- The Young Edinburgh Whigs and the Foundation of the *Edinburgh Review* 11
- First Contributions to the *Asiatic Annual Register* 13
- First Contributions to the *Edinburgh Review* and Last Contributions to the *Asiatic Annual Register* 22
- Intended Publication of a Geographical Dictionary of Asia 30

CHAPTER IV. PARIS: THE INTRODUCTION OF SANSKRIT ON THE CONTINENT 34
- Departure for Paris 34
- Prisoner of War 35
- Privileged Treatment 36
- Catalogue of Sanskrit Manuscripts in the National Library 38
- Langlès 41
- Friedrich Schlegel 44
- August Wilhelm Schlegel 52
- Hagemann 54
- Volney 54
- Fauriel 55
- Raynouard 57
- Chézy 59
- Jean-Louis Burnouf 61
- Hamilton's Role in Paris 62

CHAPTER V. EAST INDIA COLLEGE: TEACHING AND PUBLICATION OF CLASSBOOKS 64
Return to Great Britain 64
Appointment to the East India College 65
Teaching 66
Life at the College 68
Resignation from the College 69
Publication of Classbooks 72
Edition of the Hitopadeśa 73
Grammatical Analysis of the Hitopadeśa 75
Criticisms of the Edition and the Analysis of the Hitopadeśa 75
Sanskrit Grammatical Terminology 79

CHAPTER VI. ACTIVITIES OUTSIDE THE EAST INDIA COLLEGE 81
New Contributions to the *Edinburgh Review* 81
Election to the Royal Society 109
Frank and the Election to the Munich Academy 109
Journey on the Continent 111

CHAPTER VII. THE LAST YEARS 112
Bopp 112
Last Contribution to the *Edinburgh Review* 114
An Apocrypha: *A Key to the Chronology of the Hindus* 118
The Royal Asiatic Society 120
The End 120
Unknown Articles about Ancient Indian Geography 121
Unpublished Sanskrit Dictionary 121

CONCLUSION 122

INDEX NOMINUM 125

INTRODUCTION

It has been generally accepted that the birth of comparative philology in the beginning of the 19th century was due to the circumstance that the Occident became acquainted with the Sanskrit language. However, never enough moment has been attributed to the very curious fact that, whereas Indic studies practically were a monopoly of the British, the comparative method was inaugurated by Germans. In order to hold with a fair degree of probability that Sanskrit was at the very basis of comparative philology, it is of no little interest to show how, where and when the Germans were in a position to learn the prestigious speech which for a long time they considered as the mother of all Indo-European languages. It so happens that the link between British and German scholars must be looked for in Paris in the Napoleonic period and, in particular, with one single individual by the name of Alexander Hamilton.

The *Gentleman's Magazine* for February 1825 has the following obituary: "*Dec.* 30. At Liverpool, aged 62, Alex. Hamilton, esq. F. R. S., a celebrated Oriental scholar, and late Professor of Sanscrit and Hindoo Literature at the East India College, Hayleybury.—We should be grateful for a memoir of this distinguished scholar."[1] However, the latter request does not seem ever to have been fulfilled, since one vainly looks for a memoir of Hamilton in the subsequent numbers of the *Gentleman's Magazine*.

The *Edinburgh Annual Register* does mention the death of Alexander Hamilton,[2] but it does not go to the extent of publishing an actual memoir. Even worse, the *Annual Biography and Obituary*, as well as the *Annual Register*, do not know of his death at all. One thus understands the shocked surprise of the editors of the *Journal Asiatique*: "Il est assez extraordinaire qu'aucun journal anglais n'ait consacré un article nécrologique un peu étendu à la mémoire de ce savant distingué."[3]

The following pages are meant to provide a memoir of Alexander Hamilton more than 140 years after the appeal launched by the *Gentleman's Magazine*.

It is true that the various biographical dictionaries do contain notices about Hamilton,[4] but they often offer erroneous information, as will be seen on more than one occasion below. The reference works about the history of Oriental

[1] 95, 1, London, p. 189.

[2] 17, Edinburgh, 1824, p. 470.

[3] 7, Paris, October 1825, pp. 255-256.

[4] *Biographie nouvelle des contemporains* (*BNC*), Paris, 1823; *Biographie universelle ancienne et moderne* (*BU*), nouv. éd., Paris, 1857; *Nouvelle biographie générale depuis les temps les plus reculés jusqu'à nos jours* (*NBG*), Paris, 1858; *Dictionary of National Biography* (*DNB*), 2nd ed., London, 1908; and also C. E. Buckland: *Dictionary of Indian Biography* (*DIB*), London, 1906.

studies[5] again and again reproduce the same errors; moreover, they are mainly interested in Hamilton as far as his stay in Paris is concerned; apart from his catalogue of the Sanskrit manuscripts of the Imperial Library, they essentially refer to him in connection with an apparently more important Orientalist, namely the one who became Hamilton's most famous student in Paris—Friedrich Schlegel.

The only article which has ever been really devoted to Hamilton was the one by R. W. Chambers and F. Norman: *Alexander Hamilton and the Beginnings of Comparative Philology.* It is to be regretted that this paper appeared in a volume which, though of a very high standard, is not normally known to Orientalists.[6] Moreover, it is a study of only one of Hamilton's numerous articles, his review of Wilkins's Sanskrit Grammar.[7]

[5] Theodor Benfey: *Geschichte der Sprachwissenschaft und orientalischen Philologie in Deutschland seit dem Anfange des 19. Jahrhunderts mit einem Rückblick auf die früheren Zeiten*, München, 1869, pp. 357-361; James Darmesteter: *De la part de la France dans les grandes découvertes de l'orientalisme moderne*, in: *Essais orientaux*, Paris, 1883, pp. 27-28; E. Windisch: *Geschichte der Sanskrit-Philologie und Indischen Altertumskunde*, 2 vol., Strassburg, 1917—Berlin-Leipzig, 1920, vol. I, pp. 53 and 57-58; Sylvain Levi: *Les Origines d'une Chaire: l'Entrée du Sanscrit au Collège de France*, in: *Le Collège de France (1530-1930)*, Paris, 1932, pp. 329-344; H. G. Rawlinson: *India in European Literature and Thought*, in: G. T. Garratt (ed.): *The Legacy of India*, Oxford, 1937, p. 31; H. G. Rawlinson: *Indian Influence on the West*, in: L. S. S. O'Malley (ed.): *Modern India and the West*, London etc., 1941, pp. 546-547; Atul Chatterjee—Richard Burn: *British Contributions to Indian Studies*, London, [1943], p. 15; Raymond Schwab: *La renaissance orientale*, Paris, 1950, pp. 74-77 and passim; P. Masson-Oursel, H. De Willman-Grabowska, Philippe Stern: *L'Inde antique et la civilisation indienne*, Paris, 1951, p. 265; A. L. Basham: *The Wonder that was India*, London, [1954], p. 6.

[6] In: *Studies in English Philology. A Miscellany in honor of Frederick Klaeber*, Minneapolis, 1929, pp. 457-466.

[7] In: *Edinburgh Review* (*Ed. Rev.*) 13, Edinburgh, January 1809, pp. 366-381.

CHAPTER I

THE EARLY YEARS

Alexander Hamilton was born in 1762.[1] It is not known where he was born, nor who his parents were.[2] All we know is that he was a Scotsman,[3] but not a native of Edinburgh.[4] It seems he did not belong to the famous Hamilton family; at least he does not figure among the many Alexanders who are listed in the index to George Hamilton's *History of the House of Hamilton,* although in his preface the author explicitly states that the said index includes "Hamilton males, of past generations, of whom something substantial is known, whether by way of rank, territorial cognomen, profession or trade."[5]

The only reference to a member of Alexander Hamilton's family is given by Langlès, according to whom Walter Hamilton, the author of the *East India Gazetteer* and of the *Geographical, Statistical, and Historical Description of Hindostan, and the Adjacent Countries* was his brother. In his review of the former book, Langlès says: "Pourquoi tairois-je une circonstance qui accroît à mes yeux le vif intérêt que ce savant doit généralement exciter; il est à tous égards le digne frère de M. Alexandre Hamilton . . . ," and further:

[1] We do not know of any document directly attesting this date; it has merely been inferred from the fact that Hamilton was aged 62 when he died on December 30, 1824, according to the obituary of the *Gentleman's Magazine* cited above. In any case, there is no ground to pose 1765 as the year of his birth, as in BENFEY: *op. cit.*, p. 358, and Rudolf UNGER (ed.): *Briefe von Dorothea und Friedrich Schlegel an die Familie Paulus* (= *Deutsche Literaturdenkmale des 18. und 19. Jahrhunderts*, 146. Dritte Folge, 26), Berlin, 1913, p. 128. The *NBG* also situates Hamilton's birth around 1765.

[2] It is characteristic that nothing on that subject appears in V. C. P. HODSON: *List of the Officers of the Bengal Army 1758-1834. Alphabetically Arranged with Biographical and Genealogical Notices*, 4 vol., London, 1927-1947, although this work normally does contain such information whenever it is known. In F. BAETHGEN (ed.): *Geist und Gestalt. Biographische Beiträge zur Geschichte der Bayerischen Akademie der Wissenschaften vornehmlich im zweiten Jahrhundert ihres Bestehens,* München, 1959–, Ergänzungsband, Erste Hälfte: U. THUERAUF: *Gesamtverzeichnis der Mitglieder der Bayerischen Akademie der Wissenschaften in den ersten beiden Jahrhunderten ihres Bestehens 1759-1959,* p. 63, the mention: "Hamilton Alexander, * 1762 Liverpool, † 1824" must be regarded as resulting from a confusion with the place of his death.

[3] Lord COCKBURN: *Life of Lord Jeffrey,* 2nd ed., 2 vol., Edinburgh, 1852, vol. I, p. 141; Helmine von CHEZY: *Ueberlieferungen und Umrisse aus den Tagen Napoleons. 3. Friedrich und Dorothea von Schlegel in Paris,* in: *Freihafen* III, 4, Altona, 1840, p. 85.

[4] Lord COCKBURN: *Life of Lord Jeffrey,* vol. I, p. 107.

[5] Edinburgh, 1933, p. VIII.

"Ainsi une heureuse sympathie a dirigé l'attention des deux frères vers l'Inde, dont l'un exploite depuis longtemps les innombrables et antiques richesses littéraires, l'autre recueille avec soin et discernement les notions géographiques les plus utiles et les plus authentiques, auxquelles il ajoute ses propres observations sur la même contrée. Le premier s'acquiert des droits à la reconnoissance de ses lecteurs, l'autre à celle de ses auditeurs, comme ils en ont tous deux à l'estime de ceux qui les connoissent."[6] We have not been able to find confirmation for this assertion elsewhere, but, given Langlès's very intimate friendship with Alexander Hamilton, we must accept it as probable. Moreover, Langlès does not seem to have been contradicted by either Hamilton on that point, since ten years later he again writes that Walter Hamilton is a "digne frère de mon savant ami M. Alexandre Hamilton."[7]

From the fact that Hamilton's father was able to secure an Indian career for two sons, we dare infer that he was at least a person of some importance. Moreover, as we shall see later, after his father's death, Dorothea Schlegel speaks of Alexander Hamilton as a rich man.

We are left completely in the dark as to what and where Alexander Hamilton studied; the only data in this respect are to be drawn from a reference he himself makes at a later stage to a tolerable knowledge of Latin, and a slender knowledge of Greek.[8] Our efforts to trace his presence in any British University at the time did not meet with success, at least not from the various catalogues of graduates we consulted at the British Museum. There is one Alexander Hamilton who obtained a B. A. degree in the University of Dublin in the Spring of 1783,[9] but there is no reason to identify the holder of this Irish degree with the Scottish Alexander Hamilton we are concerned with.

[6] *Notice de l'ouvrage intitulé: The East India Gazetteer, etc.*, in: *Magasin Encyclopédique*, Paris, August 1815, pp. 11-12 of the offprint.

[7] *Analyse des Mémoires contenus dans le XIVe volume des Asiatick Researches*, Paris, 1825, p. 63, n. 2.

[8] Review of Wilkins's Sanskrit Grammar, in: *Ed. Rev.* 13, January 1809, p. 371. His knowledge of Greek does not however prove to be as slender as one might expect from this quotation.

[9] *A Catalogue of Graduates who have proceeded to degrees in the University of Dublin from the earliest recorded commencements to July, 1866*, Dublin, 1869.

CHAPTER II

CALCUTTA: THE DISCOVERY OF SANSKRIT

THE BENGAL ARMY

In 1783, the very year in which Sir William Jones was sent to Calcutta as a judge, Hamilton obtained a cadetship for the Bengal Army.[1] Whereas it is specifically known that Sir William Jones arrived in December 1783, there is again no indication about the date of Hamilton's arrival in Calcutta.[2] At any rate, it cannot have taken place before the end of 1783.

Hamilton received his first commission early in 1785; he became an ensign in the infantry,[3] on February 22 according to some sources,[4] on March 13 according to others.[5] From 1785 to 1790, Hamilton remained supernumerary; under the title "Ensigns Supernumerary to the Establishment, To be brought from the 15th February 1790, on Full Pay and Posted to Corps," the *Bengal Calendar and Register* for 1790 lists "Alexander Hamilton 3d. Bat. 1st. Brig. Nat. Inf."[6] However, this assignment seems to have been modified even before it took effect, since the *Calcutta Monthly Register* mentions, under the date of February 15, 1790, that "Ensign A. Hamilton supernumerary to the establishment, has been brought on full pay from this day, and posted to the fourth European battalion,"[7] a decision which was postponed until June 12, 1790, when the same source reports: "Ens. A. Hamilton, removed from supernumerary to the 4th Eur. bat. *vice* Dalston."[8]

THE DISCOVERY OF SANSKRIT

Meanwhile, the young ensign availed himself of his stay in Calcutta to study the languages and culture of India. This interest arose very soon, since

[1] DODWELL—MILES: *Alphabetical List of the Officers of the Indian Army with the dates of their respective promotion, retirement, resignation, or death, whether in India or in Europe; from the year 1760, to the year 1834 inclusive, corrected to September 30, 1837*, London, 1838; HODSON: *op. cit.*

[2] An indication which is given by HODSON whenever it is known.

[3] The erroneous mention of Hamilton as an officer in the navy in S. LEFMANN: *Franz Bopp*, 3 vol., Berlin, 1891-1897, p. 18, Nachtrag, p. XXXII, has been repeated by WINDISCH: *op. cit.*, vol. I, p. 57; LEVI: *op. cit.*, p. 338; SCHWAB: *op. cit.*, p. 74.

[4] DODWELL—MILES: *op. cit.; Bengal Calendar*, Calcutta, 1788, p. 32.

[5] HODSON: *op. cit.; Bengal Register*, Calcutta, 1787, p. 22; *Bengal Calendar and Register*, Calcutta, 1790, p. 19 of the list of infantry ensigns.

[6] P. 7 of the additions.

[7] I, 1, Calcutta, November 1790, p. 53.

[8] *Ibid.*, p. 55.

his name is found among the early members of the Asiatic Society. The exact date of his admission to the Society is not known. At any rate—whether or not he was already present in Calcutta on January 15, 1784—Hamilton did not attend the memorable meeting held on the day when Sir William Jones founded the Asiatic Society; he consequently did not belong to the founding members of the Society.[9] However, he became a member soon after, since the first list, published in volume one of the *Asiatick Researches* which enumerates all members from January 15, 1784 to January 15, 1789, includes: "Lieut. Alexander Hamilton."[10]

More important than the exact date of his admission is the fact that Hamilton soon joined the intellectual elite who passionately studied Indian culture and subsequently revealed it to the rest of the world. It should be noted, however, that Hamilton was merely a passive member of the Asiatic Society; he never contributed to the *Asiatick Researches* an article of his own.[11] Actually, this fact should not surprise us; throughout his life, his interest in Sanskrit was restricted mainly to reading and to discussions with friends; he all too rarely went so far as to put his ideas down in writing, and, to the continuous despair of his biographer, he never added his name to the contributions he did publish.

It would be of considerable interest to know whether, like Sir William Jones, Hamilton already had any notions of oriental languages before going to India, or whether it was only there that he learned Sanskrit, Persian, Arabic and Bengali, the four languages he knew so well on his return to the West. Sanskrit at least he could not have learned beforehand; nevertheless it is Sanskrit which was to become his great passion. We must, therefore, assume that, as Wilkins had done before, Hamilton, too, must have found a pandit who introduced him to the language. Actually, at that time this was the only possible way, since the College of Fort William was not to be founded until 1800.

Learning Sanskrit became the main goal of Hamilton's stay in Calcutta, to such a degree that on March 4, 1790, he wrote a letter to Lord Cornwallis asking for facilities in that respect. This letter—the only one—has been preserved among the Cornwallis Papers in the Public Record Office in London. In view of its uniqueness and the particular light it throws upon Hamilton's character, we shall reproduce it here in extenso:

[9] Cf. *Centenary Review of the Asiatic Society of Bengal. From 1784 to 1883*, Calcutta, 1885, p. 3. BASHAM: *op. cit.*, p. 6 is not completely correct on this point.

[10] Calcutta, 1788, p. 440.

[11] Cf. *Centenary Review of the Asiatic Society of Bengal*, pp. 106-195: *Index to the Papers and Contributions to the Asiatick Researches and the Journal and Proceedings of the Asiatic Society of Bengal.*

"My Lord.

I beg leave to submit in the most respectful manner to your Lordship's consideration, a request which I flatter myself will not be deemed unreasonable, when the motives upon which it is founded are considered. A sense of the utility which might be derived from a knowledge of the Sungscrit language, its importance to the political interests of England in this country, and the conviction of that importance discovered by the Court of Directors in their approbation of the ample salary granted to Mr. Wilkins during the crisis of last war to enable him to prosecute that study, as well as in the letter from their Chairman, congratulating that Gentleman on so extraordinary an attainment, encouraged me to engage in a pursuit, where my own inclination was stimulated by so flattering a precedent. The liberal and enlightened policy of the Honble Court could not fail to suggest to them the difficulty of governing a nation, without an intimate acquaintance with its language, religion, laws, manners and customs: and that with respect to the Hindûs who constitute the great body of the people, and who from their superiority in mental endowments as well as in industry and number, merit the first consideration, that knowledge is chiefly to be expected from the development of the science contained in their Sacred Language. Whether these, or motives more cogent influenced the Court of Directors I shall not presume to determine; it is sufficient for my purpose to shew by a respectful reference to that document, that it was their wish to encourage the study, and that such a resolution was founded on the wisest principles of policy. A due regard for your Lordship's time will not permit me to encroach on it so far as would be requisite to prove how essentially the knowledge, to which those researches ultimately tend, is connected with the happiness of the subject and the security of property. The importance of the Sungscrit in a political view requires no elucidation, it being the only language universally diffused over every part of Hindustan, by means of which the Bramins of Bengal, Mysore, Guzerat or the Punjab possess a common medium of communication and intercourse, and from which the vernacular dialects of the Provinces do not materially differ. If those observations which I have purposely compressed convince your Lordship of the superior utility of my present pursuits, I may flatter myself I shall experience no difficulty in obtaining a dispensation from military duty at least whilst I continue supernumerary to the Army Establishment. The routine of Garrison duty being altogether incompatible with similar pursuits I may urge my request on different grounds, as the convenience it affords me of indulging my inclination in the research, is my chief if not my sole motive for continuing in a Service, where I have no prospect of attaining beyond the situation of a Subaltern. Should the exemption I most humbly solicit still appear objectionable, I may yet hope your Lordship will not class this application with those which motives of interest or pecuniary convenience may have produced from others.—I have the honour to be.

My Lord.

Your Lordships most obedt
and very humble Servt
A. Hamilton

Calcutta 4th March

P. S. It appears totally superfluous to add that my request does not extend to an exemption from real service, but to the ordinary routine of Garrison duty exclusively.

To Earl Cornwallis. K. G." [12]

RESIGNATION FROM THE ARMY

We have not been able to discover any kind of reply to Hamilton's request to Cornwallis. However, we do know that Hamilton, who, as said above, ceased to be supernumerary on June 12, 1790, soon resigned from the army. The *Calcutta Monthly Register* for October 1790, without however stating the exact date—October 6, according to Hodson [13]—, mentions: "Ensign Alexander Hamilton, having received permission to resign the service, at his own request, his name is struck off the List of the Army." [14] This resignation is also attested by the 2nd volume of the *Asiatick Researches*; in the list of members of the Asiatic Society at the end of the year 1790, Hamilton is now indicated as "Alex. Hamilton. Esq." [15]

Hamilton's decision to leave the army would normally lead us to the conclusion that his former request to Lord Cornwallis had met with a refusal. However, a refusal of Lord Cornwallis would be astonishing, at a time when he offered rewards and facilities to the civil servants who engaged in learning oriental languages. Moreover, there is another possibility. Lord Cockburn, who was personally acquainted with Hamilton after the latter's return home, makes the interesting remark that "he was secretary to Lord Cornwallis." [16] It is to be regretted that Lord Cockburn does not say anything as to where and when Hamilton held this post. However, looking at Hamilton's biography as a whole we must come to the conclusion that the only period during which this might have taken place is the one between 1790 and 1800. Indeed, this

[12] *PRO* 30/11, bundle 148, leaf 82. The transcript of this Crown-copyright record appears by permission of the Controller of H. M. Stationery Office.

[13] *Op. cit.*

[14] I, 1, November 1790, p. 58.

[15] Calcutta, 1790, p. 502.

[16] *An Account of the Friday Club*, in: *The Book of the Old Edinburgh Club*, vol. III, Edinburgh, 1910, p. 114.

is the only decade of Hamilton's life during which we could not trace any of his activities, nor even his place of residence. Unfortunately we have not been able to find any direct confirmation of Lord Cockburn's notice, at least not in the published materials in connection with Lord Cornwallis; perhaps it may be hoped that such a confirmation will be found one day in the vast amount of surviving manuscript materials about this period of Indian history. Notwithstanding all this we are inclined to give full credit to the above statement on the ground that Lord Cockburn, a close friend of Hamilton, must have been well informed. It seems probable to us that Lord Cornwallis, perhaps on the recommendation of one of Hamilton's distinguished fellow-members of the Asiatic Society, offered him a position which better fitted his inclination towards research than a military post on the eve of the war against Tipu Sultan.

It should also be noticed that in later years Hamilton constantly supported the measures taken by Cornwallis for the settlement of revenue in Bengal. This appears, for instance, from his review of Wilks's *Historical Sketches of the South of India*, where he thus explains his strong adherence to Cornwallis's measures against Wilks's criticisms: "To conclude, we are sensible that, in venturing to combat some of the opinions of a writer, who, in addition to the talents, of which this work exhibits ample proof, possesses a local knowledge of the state of society in the peninsula of India, we may justly be accused of presumption. Our confidence in general principles, and our recollection of the facts discovered in the course of the inquiries, preparatory to the permanent settlement of the revenues in Bengal, has perhaps encouraged us to assert, where we should only have stated our doubts."[17]

We have no indication of the exact date of Hamilton's departure from India. The *Bengal Kalendar and Almanack*, published in Calcutta in 1792, does not mention him at all, either in the military and civil list of the Company's servants, or in the list of the British residents who were not in the service of the Company. This does not, however, necessarily mean that he had indeed left India; he would not be mentioned in the first two categories, since he was no longer a Company servant, and the third list essentially contains merchants and craftsmen who worked in Calcutta. Even if Hamilton was still in Calcutta at the time, it should be no surprise not to find him in these lists; he would not have fitted in any of the three categories.

Two items of indirect testimony lead to the conclusion that Hamilton did stay on in India for several years. They even imply that he did not return to Great Britain at the same time as Cornwallis, in October 1793.

The first item comes from Hamilton himself. He writes: "In 1793 the late Mr. Hiram Cox and Doctor Charles Campbell travelled through the central mountains of the island (= Sumatra) at the imminent hazard of their lives. It was, from frequent conversations with these gentlemen, that we

[17] In: *Ed. Rev.* 18, August 1811, p. 369.

derived our information on this point."[18] On the other hand, we know that Hiram Cox never returned to England;[19] the conversations alluded to must therefore have taken place in India, at the end of 1793 or thereafter.

The second item comes from Helmine von Chezy, who lived in the house of the Schlegels in Paris at the same time as Hamilton, and who is one of our most valuable sources as far as Hamilton's personal life is concerned. In an often quoted passage from her autobiography, she says: "der berühmte Indianist Hamilton, der Ostindien viele Jahre lang bewohnt und dort eine Eingeborene zur Gattin und einen hoffnungsvollen Sohn besass."[20] But she gives much more detailed information in one of her other writings, which is less known: "Sein Herz war in Indien geblieben, wo ihn zarte, heilige Bande dreizehn Jahr lang beglückt, er hatte eine Eingeborne zur Ehe genommen, und einen Sohn von ihr, oft sprach er von seinem Bunde mit diesem süssen Geschöpf, mit jener, ich möchte sagen, verschämten Rührung und Innigkeit, die ein Wahrzeichen der Aechtheit eines tiefen Gefühls."[21]

The important element in this passage is that, according to Helmine von Chezy, Hamilton would have been married for thirteen years before he left India. Assuming that he could not have come to India before the end of 1783, and allowing some time before he decided to marry an Indian woman, one may conclude that he cannot have left India before the year 1797. It is the more interesting to arrive at the year 1797 as the *terminus post quem* for his departure from India, because the year 1797 at the same time is the *terminus post quem* given by another source for his arrival in Edinburgh. Indeed, according to a statement of Lord Cockburn: "In particular, between 1797 and 1800, some conspicuous young men had come to Edinburgh, to whom, being strangers, the merits of Jeffrey were more apparent than they hitherto had been to many of those among whom he dwelt. Some of these have been already named in mentioning the Speculative Society . . . In addition to these were Lord Webb Seymour, Mr. Sydney Smith, and Mr. Hamilton, also strangers."[22]

[18] Review of *Asiatick Researches*, vol. 6, in: *Asiatic Annual Register* 4, for the Year 1802, 1803, Account of Books, p. 20, n.

[19] Cf. preface to H. C. M. Cox (ed.): *Journal of a Residence in the Burmham Empire*, London, 1821.

[20] *Unvergessenes*, 2 vol., Leipzig, 1858, vol. I, p. 270.

[21] *Ueberlieferungen und Umrisse aus den Tagen Napoleons*, in: *Freihafen* III, 4, 1840, p. 86. This proves the error of the conclusion drawn by some authors from the preceding testimony, according to which Hamilton would have been accompanied by his wife and son in Paris. Cf. John Goldworth ALGER: *Napoleon's British Visitors and Captives 1801-1815*, Westminster, 1904, p. 89: "He took with him his Creole wife and a promising son"; LEVI: *op. cit.*, p. 338: "Hamilton vint donc à Paris, sans aucune préoccupation, amenant sa femme, une indigène qu'il avait épousée au Bengale, et son jeune fils." Moreover, we shall see that in all sources concerning his European period Hamilton is spoken of as living alone.

[22] *Life of Lord Jeffrey*, vol. I, p. 107.

CHAPTER III

GREAT BRITAIN: THE FIRST PUBLICATIONS

THE YOUNG EDINBURGH WHIGS AND THE FOUNDATION OF THE *EDINBURGH REVIEW*

After his return from the East Hamilton settled in Edinburgh, where he became a member of the group of young Whigs who gathered around Francis Jeffrey. Among these brilliant young men, Hamilton was obviously very much appreciated, and all references to his name are invariably accompanied by tokens of warm friendship. Thus the description which Lord Cockburn gives of him: "Mr. Hamilton was a Scotchman, who had been in India, a little, amiable person, of excellent conversation, and great knowledge of Oriental literature."[1] And yet, this description is somewhat academic; in fact, no member of the group would call him Mr. Hamilton, nor even Alexander Hamilton: instead they give him nicknames, such as "Sanscrit Hamilton," or "the Pundit." In their minds Hamilton and Sanskrit had become inseparable, and this fact made a deep impression upon them, as is clear from this curious extract of a letter written by Jeffrey to Morehead, where he thus expresses how much his own wife means to him: "But she is my brother and sister, my father and mother, my Sanscrit, my Sydney (= Sydney Smith), and my right venerable cousin, as old Homer says in Andromache."[2]

Jeffrey and Hamilton became such close friends that, during the autumn of 1800, they made plans for a voyage together: "During the autumn of this year, he and his friend Sanscrit Hamilton planned an expedition to Germany. 'We propose to make a philosophical tour into the southern parts of the empire, observing men, women and minerals, and journeying with the simple economy of the sages and apostles of old.' But it was soon found that even this apostolic pilgrimage would require a hundred guineas, and 'I have not twenty in the world.' (To John, 17th June 1800)."[3]

The group of young Edinburgh Whigs was soon to become famous when Jeffrey and his friends started the well known *Edinburgh Review*. Hamilton was among the very first who knew of the plan: "This Review was concerted, about the end of last winter, between Jeffrey, Sydney Smith, and myself. The

[1] *Life of Lord Jeffrey*, vol. I, p. 141.

[2] *Ibid.*, vol. II, p. 65. This letter is dated May 24, 1802.

[3] *Ibid.*, vol. I, p. 115.

plan was immediately communicated to Murray, Allen, and Hamilton; Brown, Brougham, and the two Thomsons, have gradually been made parties." [4]

Hamilton thus undoubtedly belonged to a very distinguished company. Lord Cockburn introduced the names of the contributors in the following terms: "The mere mention of the names of a few of those who addressed the public through this organ, during Jeffrey's editorship, is of itself sufficient to attest the high character of the instruction given, and to guarantee its safety. How could a periodical work be but magnificent, of which it could be said that it was carried on by such men as the following, all in the full force of their powers, and each zealous on his favourite subject," and, among the names enumerated, figures "Alexr. (Sanscrit) Hamilton." [5]

During the difficult start which the editors had to face, Hamilton seems to have been one of the most reliable contributors: "I must first tell you about the Review though, that you may be satisfied it holds the first place in my affection. We are in a miserable state of backwardness, you must know, and have been giving some symptoms of despondency; various measures have been tried, at least, against the earliness of our intended day of publication; and hints have been given of a delay that I am afraid would prove fatal. Something is done, however, and a good deal, I hope, is doing. Smith has gone through more than half his task. So has Hamilton. Allen has made some progress: and Murray and myself, I believe, have studied our parts, and tuned our instruments, and are *almost ready to begin*." [6]

The greatest problem for present day research on the *Edinburgh Review* is that no article bears the name of its author; it is therefore extremely difficult to single out Hamilton's articles. We have nevertheless tried to do so, but we are by no means sure that we have really succeeded in bringing all of them together. In doing so, we have derived some help from the work of W. A. Copinger: *On the Authorship of the First Hundred Numbers of the "Edinburgh Review*." [7] It should be noted, however, that this book does not contain a complete list of all articles: numerous articles have not been attributed to any author. Moreover, we fear that it is not free from erroneous attributions. And, finally, the author unfortunately neglected to state how he proceeded to ascertain the authorship. In compensation we were lucky to find that some contributors to the *Edinburgh Review* published lists of their articles; the correspondence between the editors has also proved a valuable source of information.

In some cases, it is evident that the review cannot have been written by

[4] Leonard HORNER (ed.): *Memoirs and Correspondence of Francis Horner*, 2nd ed., 2 vol., Boston—London, 1853, vol. I, p. 209; this extract from Francis Horner's memoirs is dated September 30, 1802.

[5] *Life of Lord Jeffrey*, vol. I, pp. 300-301.

[6] *Ibid.*, vol. I, p. 186; from a letter addressed by Jeffrey to Horner, April 9, 1802.

[7] *Bibliographiana* 2, Manchester, 1895.

anybody but Hamilton himself; for instance, when Sanskrit takes the first place. In other cases, however, the doubt remains; one should indeed keep in mind that Hamilton may have written articles which are not at all about India, and wherein consequently nothing points to him as the author. Anyhow, for each of the numerous articles we shall analyze throughout this work, we shall mention all the arguments which make us believe that it may be attributed to Hamilton.

FIRST CONTRIBUTIONS TO THE *ASIATIC ANNUAL REGISTER*

Hamilton's contributions to the *Edinburgh Review* do not constitute his first attempts at writing articles. Before the foundation of the *Edinburgh Review,* he indeed contributed several papers to the *Asiatic Annual Register.* All these contributions are, once again, anonymous, although this was not a rule in the *Asiatic Annual Register.*

If it is not always easy to ascertain Hamilton's authorship of articles in the *Edinburgh Review,* the difficulty is still greater with regard to the *Asiatic Annual Register.* Here, we do not possess any secondary information such as correspondence or lists of articles. Moreover, if Hamilton was the only contributor to the *Edinburgh Review* who knew Sanskrit, this can hardly be supposed to have been the case with regard to an oriental journal such as the *Asiatic Annual Register.* As a matter of fact, it was in Hamilton's contributions to the *Edinburgh Review* that we came across references to earlier articles of his in the *Asiatic Annual Register.* Since these references did not mention the specific volumes of the *Asiatic Annual Register* in which they appeared, we thought it necessary to go through all the—badly indexed—volumes; and in doing so after having read Hamilton's numerous contributions to the *Edinburgh Review,* we recognized Hamilton's style in other articles published in the *Asiatic Annual Register.* In some cases, no doubt is possible; in some others, we cannot be sure that Hamilton was the author. We shall only mention here those articles which are undoubtedly his. We are nevertheless convinced that Hamilton contributed a great many articles to the *Asiatic Annual Register*; we are even inclined to admit that he did have some responsibility in the editorial work.

The *Asiatic Annual Register,* of which the first volume appeared in 1800, dealt with any kind of subject relating to India, India meaning at the time the East Indies, *i. e.* South East Asia as well. It published a history of British India, intelligence about occurrences in India; it discussed State Papers about India, and it recorded debates in Parliament and at the East India House. As far as concerns such topics as these we do not think that Hamilton was ever associated with them. But it also published Miscellaneous Tracts, both original and reprinted from journals published in India, both signed and anonymous, dealing with various aspects of Indian culture; finally it also contained reviews of books concerning all facets of India. In these latter two sections, we are of the opinion that Hamilton took a great part, both in writing articles and in selecting suitable papers for publication. Indeed, some articles of which he undoubtedly was the author establish a relationship between his reviews and extracts from the books reproduced in the *Asiatic Annual Register.* The following passages may be cited as illustrations: "Our philosophic readers might expect a more particular account of a people thus singularly circumstanced, had we not extracted the entire passage, in our last volume"; [8] "On these it were superfluous to enlarge, having inserted the chapter entire in our last volume"; [9] "In our Register for the year 1800, we inserted entire, four of the most interesting tracts in the volume now before us." [10]

The first issue of the *Asiatic Annual Register* which bears the name of an editor, Lawrence Dundas Campbell, is volume 6, published in 1806, at a time when Hamilton had left Great Britain for Paris. As will be seen later, the preface to this volume may contain an allusion to Hamilton's departure, which caused additional problems for the editor.

The two articles of Hamilton to which references are made in his contributions to the *Edinburgh Review* appeared in the second volume of the *Asiatic Annual Register.*

Two articles in the *Edinburgh Review* which, as will be seen later, must be attributed to Hamilton, mention a translation of his in the *Asiatic Annual Register* of a Persian description of Vijayanagar written by the ambassador of Mirza Shahrukh and inserted in Khondamir's Habib al-siyar.[11] The second volume of the *Asiatic Annual Register* indeed contains an article entitled: *An Account of the Cities of Calicut and Bijanagar in the 15th Century, translated from the Persic of Khondemir, with Explanatory Notes.*[12] Since the article itself consists in a translation of a Persian text, only the notes are original contributions, which give us an idea of Hamilton's personal opinions. These notes are very interesting indeed, and they already announce the main themes and the specific preoccupations which Hamilton developed in his later works. The article being primarily concerned with a Persian text, the numerous references to Sanskrit texts and to Sanskrit terms are the more remarkable. His two favourite topics throughout his whole life—ancient Indian geography, and comparative mythology—already come to the fore.

[8] Review of Symes's *Account of an Embassy to the Kingdom of Ava,* in: *Asiatic Annual Register* 3, for the Year 1801, London, 1802, Account of Books, p. 23.

[9] *Ibid.*, p. 28.

[10] Review of *Asiatick Researches,* vol. 6, in: *Asiatic Annual Register* 4, for the Year 1802, 1803, Account of Books, p. 18.

[11] Review of Buchanan's *Journey from Madras,* in: *Ed. Rev.* 13, October 1808, p. 84; Review of Wilks's *Historical Sketches of the South of India,* in: *Ed. Rev.* 18, August 1811, pp. 356-357.

[12] For the Year 1800, 1801, Miscellaneous Tracts, pp. 226-231.

Hamilton makes a point of identifying the old city corresponding to modern Bijanagar:

"Bijanagur is confounded with Bijapur by the late Mr. Chambers, who has favoured the public with a translation of the curious correspondence between Mirza Shahrockh and the Emperor of China; by Mr. Anderson, in his account of Malabar, it is said to be the same with Golconda . . . Vijaya (invincible) is a common Sanscreet appellation both for persons and places: this the Moslems have corrupted to Bija; and the site of this once splendid city is marked on most maps by the still more erroneous appellation of Bisnagar."[13]

As far as comparative mythology is concerned, Hamilton avails himself of every opportunity to identify Hindu deities with Greek and Roman gods:

"Calicut and Calcutta is the same word, though differently pronounced by foreigners; the latter derives its name from a temple of Cali, the Indian Hecate, situated at the distance of two miles."[14]

He also for the first time attests here his marked preference for Hindu as compared to Moslem institutions:

"This incidental remark betrays the vast inferiority of the police and government in Moslem states to those which prevailed under Hindu governments. An inhabitant of the most polished state in Persia was astonished, at Bijanagur, to perceive private merchants venture to display their riches, without dreading the cupidity of courtiers, or the depredation of the populace."[15]

In two articles in the *Edinburgh Review* Hamilton also refers to another earlier translation of his in the *Asiatic Annual Register*, namely an English rendering of an account of Haidar's life from a Persian manuscript by a native of Hyderabad.[16] This appeared indeed in the second volume of the *Asiatic Annual Register*, together with translations of two other accounts of Haidar's life, under the title: *Three Biographical Memoirs, designed to illustrate the Rise of Hyder Ally Khan, the first Mohammedan who ruled in Mysore; to which are subjoined, Explanatory Notes.*[17] Interesting data may be drawn from Hamilton's notes to these three memoirs. Here is a sample of his sound insight in philological studies, at a time when the techniques of comparison had not yet been developed:

[13] *Ibid.*, p. 227, n.

[14] *Ibid.*, p. 226, n.

[15] *Ibid.*, p. 228, n.

[16] Review of Stewart's *Catalogue of the Oriental Library of Tippoo Sultan*, in: *Ed. Rev.* 14, July 1809, p. 324; Review of Wilks's *Historical Sketches of the South of India*, in: *Ed. Rev.* 18, August 1811, p. 354.

[17] For the Year 1800, 1801, Characters, pp. 1-10.

"The word 'Naïc' has been supposed by Mr. Moore to have the same relation to Naiket, that 'Naïb' has to Naibet. Here it must be remarked, that Naïc is a Sanscrit, Naïb an Arabic term; these languages have not the most distant analogy in their rules of derivation, nor is there any such word as Naicat. Naïc, in Sanscrit, signifies an officer or commander."[18]

In this article too, Hamilton identifies Indian and Latin deities:

"Srirunga-puttun has not existed as a capital quite two centuries. It derives its name from the temple of Srirunga, (the beautiful Sri, goddess of abundance, the Ceres of the ancient mythology of Europe.) Puttun is the manner in which the Persians write the Sanscrit word Patana, a city. Seringapatam, a further corruption, is now justified by universal usage,"[19]

and further:

"In Sanscrit, dipo signifies a light or lamp, and dipoc a bestower of light. If the word be dhipoc, it has a reference to the mystic flame which consumes the body of the Indian Cupid."[20]

As far as the identification of ancient geographical data is concerned, he displays remarkable prudence; he cannot but feel sceptical about Wilford's hypotheses, a distrust which is to grow with time:

"The Crisna, or black river, is synonymous with Cali, which Lieut. Wilford imagines to be the Nile, to the banks of which he traces various emigrations of Hindus at a distant period. Crisna is specially mentioned as one of the epithets of the Cali. Might it not be adviseable to investigate whether the local peculiarities of the Cali of the Puranas could be discovered on or near the banks of the Crisna, in the Deccan, before penetrating at once into the remote wilds of Abyssinia?"[21]

Besides these translations of Persian texts, the contributions of Hamilton to the *Asiatic Annual Register*, which we could ascertain to be his, are book-reviews. The very first volume contains at least two.

The review of Anquetil-Duperron's book about the politics and commerce of India[22] is Hamilton's, since the reviewer of Anquetil-Duperron's *Oupnekhat* in the *Asiatic Annual Register*, who, as will be seen later, undoubtedly is Hamilton, acknowledges that he had written this first review.

Hamilton shares the diffidence prevailing at the time with regard to Anquetil-Duperron's pioneer work:

[18] *Ibid.*, p. 3, n.
[19] *Ibid.*, p. 4 n.
[20] *Ibid.*, p. 4, n.
[21] *Ibid.*, p. 2, n.
[22] For the Year 1799, 1800, Account of Books, pp. 251-252.

"M. ANQUETIL DU PERRON is well known to Oriental scholars, as the author of the ZENDAVESTA, or the writings attributed to ZOROASTER, which have long since been proved to be altogether spurious. He is also author of some books on Asiatic literature, which possess less ingenuity, but infinitely more merit than the ZENDAVESTA. He is a man of splendid talents, but of little sagacity, of much sprightliness, but of slender judgment, and of various acquirements, but of no great depth of knowledge. Nevertheless he has been for many years justly esteemed one of the first Orientalists in France; and his own researches in Hindustân, no less than the admirable edition which he has given of Father TIEFENTALLER's most valuable Geographical work, intitle him to the applause of his country, as well as to the thanks of all labourers in the arts and sciences of Asia. He is indeed often inaccurate in his statements, but his publications must be allowed to contain much useful information." [23]

The first volume of the *Asiatic Annual Register* also contains a review of the first book of Paulinus a Sancto Bartholomaeo's *Voyage to the East Indies*,[24] which we do not hesitate to attribute to Hamilton. Although there is no reference to this review in any other article, his judgment of Paulinus corresponds so perfectly to that appearing in his later writings that one cannot but conclude that they must all be attributed to the same critic. The fact is that Hamilton does not appreciate Paulinus at all. However, his unusual severity is evidently to be explained as a reaction to Paulinus's violent attacks against such scholars as William Jones and Charles Wilkins, for both of whom Hamilton professes the greatest admiration. This is clear from several passages, such as the following one, brought about by Paulinus's dating of Pāṇḍu:

"We must however contend, in opposition to the learned Carmelite, with whom we should be very glad to have an opportunity of discussing this, as well as some other questions in Indian antiquities, that Mr. Wilkins's calculation is not far wrong, and that Paolino's, therefore, is *grossly erroneous*. It is indeed a matter of mere curiosity, and of no moment to the public; but it is surely of some service to the cause of Oriental literature, to support the authority of one of its greatest ornaments, against a bold but false criticism, and to reprehend one of its most boastful votaries for his arrogant assumption." [25]

Even more vehement is his vindication of Jones in the following passage:

"In his chapter on the laws of the Indians, he commences with an historical and critical dissertation on the antiquity of the *Védas*, respecting which he again controverts the opinion of Sir WILLIAM JONES; and moreover talks of that great man, as well as of Mr. WILKINS, Mr. HALHEAD, and all the other

[23] *Ibid.*, p. 251.
[24] *Ibid.*, pp. 233-243.
[25] *Ibid.*, p. 234.

learned members of the Asiatic Society, in a strain of contumely suitable enough to the insolent dogmatism of his order, and the captious vanity of his disposition, but equally unbefitting the liberal spirit of science, and the dignified sentiments of a gentleman. Paolino may perhaps accuse us of attacking him with his own weapons; but we trust our language is as different from his, as the voice of truth is from the murmers of malice. He has thought it becoming the *meekness of his Christianity* to insult those talents which he envied; whereas we have, for the honour of literature, endeavoured to defend that genius which we admire." [26]

This is indeed the most passionate plea we have met with in Hamilton's writings.

Contending, against Paulinus, that the British do not make false pretensions when quoting information given them by learned brahmans, Hamilton recalls personal memories, which attest his friendly relations with pandits:

"*We* have very frequently conversed with the *Bràhmans at Sadras,* and must do them the justice to say, that we never found them backward in communicating information respecting their sacred writings; though they have told us, that they invariably avoided any intercourse with the Romish priests, whose prying disposition they disliked, and who, they said, '*come to India with the sole, but the hopeless view of subverting, the Brahminical faith.*'" [27]

This article also gives support to the fact, alleged by the biographical dictionaries and other secondary sources,[28] that Hamilton pursued his study of Sanskrit at the British Museum after his return from India. Indeed, he says:

"the original of the work before us, written in the Italian, appeared at Rome in 1796, since which time, it has been translated both into the Latin and German languages. A copy of the Latin edition is deposited in the British Museum," [29]

and he quotes this Latin edition:

"We shall at present only mention two very prominent passages in the Latin edition of our author's book." [30]

A note to this article also proves that Hamilton was personally acquainted with Wilkins:

[26] *Ibid.*, p. 238.
[27] *Ibid.*, p. 236.
[28] *BNC*; *BU*; *NBG*; *DNB*; also LEVI: *op. cit.*, p. 338; CHATTERJEE—BURN: *op. cit.*, p. 15; CHAMBERS-NORMAN: *op. cit.*, p. 460.
[29] *Asiatic Annual Register* 1, for the Year 1799, 1800, Account of Books, p. 233.
[30] *Ibid.*, p. 238.

"The Seiks' College at Patna was visited by Mr. Wilkins, who informs us, that their religious books are written in a dialect made up of a mixture of Sanscrêet, Persian, Arabic, and the provincial idiom of the Panjab."[31]

In his letter to Cornwallis quoted above Hamilton had already named Wilkins as his model. The friendly relations between the two men are evidenced by the constant support that Wilkins later gave Hamilton. It is also only natural that, when, in 1801, Wilkins became the librarian of the East India Company, Hamilton pursued his study of Sanskrit manuscripts at the East India Library.[32]

Concluding his review of the first book of the *Voyage to the East Indies*, Hamilton invites Paulinus to a scholarly discussion:

"Such are the contents of the first book of Paolino's Travels, which we have endeavoured to analyze with impartiality and candour, though truth and justice, in some places, compelled us to be severe. If, however, the learned Carmelite should feel himself inclined to defend those opinions of his which we have controverted, we shall be happy to insert in our next volume any communications he may favour us with; as in it we purpose to review the second book of his travels."[33]

He does not seem to have received any answer on that point.

The review of the second book of Paulinus's *Voyage to the East Indies* appeared in the second volume of the *Asiatic Annual Register*,[34] and was in much the same tone. Hamilton contends that Paulinus does not know real Sanskrit, but only the Malabar idiom. He gies various examples of Paulinus's alleged ignorance of Sanskrit, for instance in the following passages:

"It might be considered illiberal were we to insinuate that Fra Paolino did not understand a language of which he has published a grammar. It must, however, be acknowledged extremely singular, that, in proof of the above-mentioned Hindû laws, he has quoted one Sanscrit book where no such thing is to be found, and three treatises on the laws of the Buddhists, preserved in the libraries at Rome, and brought from Pegu. But the system of the Talapoins differs essentially from that of the Brahmans; can it be imagined that a Sanscrit scholar would have recourse to the former to illustrate the jurisprudence of the latter?";[35]

"his orthography is uniformly erroneous in substituting the letter D for T, and G for C; these we conceive to be the Malabar pronunciation;

[31] *Ibid.*, p. 235, n.
[32] A fact recalled in *BNC*; *BU*; *NBG*.
[33] *Asiatic Annual Register* 1, for the Year 1799, 1800, Account of Books, p. 238.
[34] For the Year 1800, 1801, Account of Books, pp. 41-46.
[35] *Ibid.*, p. 42.

but would not a Sanscrit scholar have been able to detect and avoid such inaccuracies?";[36]

"An enumeration of the signs of the Zodiac occasioned Fra Paolino to assert that Cancer has been very improperly called Carcata by Sir Wm. Jones, when he should have said Carkidaga. But Sir William did not intend to give the Malabar appellation, and is not responsible for his critic's ignorance of Sanscrit. The latter supposes that the Indian months are named from the signs. If this be the case in Malabar, (which we greatly doubt,) it is peculiar to that country."[37]

The criticisms raised in this review appeared again very often in Hamilton's articles. They continued even after he had seen in France Paulinus's Sanskrit Grammar—in this article he confesses not to have seen it yet—which was held in high esteem there. On every occasion Hamilton tried to induce his fellow-orientalists to exercise much circumspection with regard to Paulinus's authority. The fact is that Paulinus's works were far less reliable than those coming from the members of the Asiatic Society. Moreover, Paulinus had learned his Sanskrit in Malabar whereas the British had learned theirs in Calcutta. When Hamilton points to Paulinus's mistakes due to Malabar pronunciation, he is not aware of the fact that his own Sanskrit evinces many examples of misspellings due to the Bengali pronunciation. The comparison with Hamilton's other reviews of books however clearly proves that his unusual harshness vis-à-vis Paulinus should be considered as a retort to the latter's attacks against such British orientalists as William Jones and Charles Wilkins.

It should also be mentioned that from this review onward Hamilton shows his particular interest in the Purāṇas, a fact of which his later works exhibit ample proof:

"A superficial account of the festivals closes this chapter: there is room for an interesting work on this subject, which should contain extracts from the Puranas, explanatory of their origin, and the ceremonies and recitations performed at their celebration. Such an account of the Indian Fasti would indicate the source, historical or astronomical, to which the wild, but interesting fables of this antique race, must be chiefly referred."[38]

Volume 3 of the *Asiatic Annual Register* contains two book-reviews which point to each other as being written by the same author, and to which similarly reference is made in another article which undoubtedly must be attributed to Hamilton, namely the review of the sixth volume of the *Asiatick Researches*

[36] *Ibid.*, p. 42.
[37] *Ibid.*, p. 45.
[38] *Ibid.*, p. 45.

in the *Asiatic Annual Register*.[39] The two reviews concerned are that of Samuel Turner's *Account of an Embassy to Teshoo Lama, in Tibet*[40] and that of Michael Symes's *Account of an Embassy to the Kingdom of Ava*.[41]

The two works under review being similar in many respects, Hamilton's reviews are closely connected. He applauds the information contained in them and thus stresses the importance of calling to the attention of the public descriptions of unknown peoples and countries:

"To review the account of an enlightened and judicious traveller of countries previously unknown, or so imperfectly described, as to differ slightly from terra incognita, is only to furnish a copious abstract of his most prominent remarks. This duty we have endeavoured to perform, in reviewing the interesting publications of Col. Symes and Capt. Turner. To compare these with the scanty accounts supplied by preceding travellers, less qualified to form correct opinions, and in situations less calculated to afford the data requisite for that purpose, were a task slightly conducive to the interests of literature. The public are now in possession of authentic descriptions, of the principal routes to the capitals of Ava and Tibet; the manners and customs of the natives, so far as they influence their intercourse with strangers, have been amply elucidated, and much light has been thrown upon these in other particulars. The expectations which might have been formed, from the short residence of the authors in the countries they described, have been equalled and surpassed: a new and prolific source has been opened by each, to the indulgence of a rational curiosity, and the applause of the public which has already crowned their labours, is the just reward of their meritorious exertions. The sciences of geography, botany, and mineralogy, have each derived some important additions from their inquiries; but it is principally to the philosopher, engaged in contemplating the nature of man, as displayed in his actions and opinions, under every diversity of climate, government, and religious system, that travels into distant regions, supply an inexhaustible fund of materials."[42]

Both for Tibet and for Burma, Hamilton refers to Sanskrit terms and Hindu institutions as being able to elucidate the new data discovered. These are two examples from the review of Symes's work:

"Shaan, he informs us, is a term given to different nations; thus the Yudra Shan, is Siam, the Cassay-Shan, Cassay. This word is manifestly the Sanscrit Sthan, of which the Persians have made 'Stan,' the Burmans, 'Shan.'";[43]

[39] 4, for the Year 1802, 1803, Account of Books, p. 29, p. 31.

[40] In: *Asiatic Annual Register* 3, for the Year 1801, 1802, Account of Books, pp. 1-19.

[41] *Ibid.*, pp. 19-34.

[42] *Ibid.*, pp. 33-34.

[43] *Ibid.*, p. 27.

"The noble edifice of Shoemadoo Praw, or the temple of the Golden Supreme, (as Col. Symes has rendered it) attracts most notice. Shoe, he informs us, signifies 'golden'; Madoo, he considers a corruption of the Sanscrit Mahadeva and Praw, a sovereign and sacerdotal title; he appears, (somewhat fancifully) to refer to the Egyptian Phra; whence he thinks Potiphera, and even the regal title of Pharaoh, to be derived. If the word be of Pali or Sanscrit origin, we have no hesitation in pronouncing it 'Somadeva Praw' a temple of the moon."[44]

It is interesting to notice that, in his later works too, Hamilton often reacts against the tendency inaugurated by William Jones and prevalent in his time, to constantly draw Egypt into the picture.

Hamilton's contribution also goes further than merely referring to Sanskrit whenever an occasion presents itself. With regard to Tibet, for instance, he attaches to his review ". . . a few particulars, calculated to reflect some light on the ancient and modern state of that country, but which being extraneous to the review of Capt. Turner's work, we have compressed as much as perspicuity would permit."[45]

FIRST CONTRIBUTIONS TO THE *EDINBURGH REVIEW* AND LAST CONTRIBUTIONS TO THE *ASIATIC ANNUAL REGISTER*

When, in 1802, Hamilton began to write for the *Edinburgh Review*, he also continued to contribute to the *Asiatic Annual Register*. As a matter of fact, he simultaneously reviewed the same books for both journals.

We have already quoted above a letter written by Jeffrey to Horner attesting that Hamilton contributed to the very first number of the *Edinburgh Review*. Moreover, Nowell C. Smith, who edited the correspondence of Sydney Smith, another early contributor, says that Hamilton contributed to the first two numbers.[46] Judging from the contents too, it is obvious that three articles published in these two numbers could only have been written by Sanskrit Hamilton.

Copinger also attributes to Hamilton the review of Storch's *Picture of Petersburg*[47] and to Hamilton or Sydney Smith the review of Sonnini's *Travels in Greece and Turkey*.[48] It must be said that nothing in the text itself of the said reviews points to Hamilton as the author, although it is equally true that nothing contradicts such an attribution.[49]

[44] *Ibid.*, p. 25.

[45] *Ibid.*, p. 15.

[46] *Letters of Sydney Smith*, 2 vol., Oxford, 1953, vol. I, p. 157, n. 4.

[47] In: *Ed. Rev.*, vol. I, no. 2, January 1803, art. 4, pp. 305-307. Attributed to Hamilton by *WIVP*.

[48] *Ibid.*, art. 2, pp. 281-287. *WIVP*: Hamilton, prob.; or S. Smith.

[49] *WIVP* also attributes to Hamilton the reviews of Baldwin's *Political Recollections relative to Egypt* (*Ed. Rev.*, vol. I, no. 1, October 1802, art. 6, pp. 59-61) and of

The review of Olivier's *Travels in the Ottoman Empire* in the *Edinburgh Review* [50] is certainly by Hamilton. Various favorite themes of his are present here: his interest in geography, the importance of studying oriental languages before attempting to write about the East, the higher degree of civilization of Hindus as compared to Muslims. There is also a reference to Abdur-Razzaq's visit as an ambassador to Vijayanagar, a parallel of which has been mentioned above.

Two articles which were undoubtedly published by Hamilton in the first two numbers of the *Edinburgh Review* have their exact counterparts in the *Asiatic Annual Register*. Among the contributors to the *Edinburgh Review*, only Hamilton could have written the reviews of the sixth volume of the *Asiatick Researches* [51] and of Anquetil-Duperron's *Oupnekhat*; [52] both articles are also attributed to Hamilton by Copinger.[53] Early in 1803 the *Asiatic Annual Register* published reviews of Anquetil-Duperron's *Oupnekhat* [54] and of part of the sixth volume of the *Asiatick Researches*,[55] this latter review being continued in the following volume.[56] The reviews published in the two journals give the most unequivocal proof that they are by one and the same author. We shall therefore analyze them simultaneously in the two journals.

The most striking fact which emerges from a comparison between the two reviews of Anquetil-Duperron's *Oupnekhat* is that the one in the *Asiatic Annual Register* is more severe than the one in the *Edinburgh Review*. Fundamentally however they reproduce the same arguments. Both reviews praise Anquetil's knowledge of Persian; in the *Edinburgh Review* Hamilton expresses his appreciation in the following terms:

"We have been so fortunate as to procure a copy of the Persic work, and having collated a great variety of passages with M. Anquetil's translation, are happy to do justice to its accuracy, and to add our testimony to the very complete knowledge of the Persic he has exhibited throughout his work." [57]

The two articles give the reviewer's translation of the preface to the Persian text, the two translations being identical word by word. Whereas this translation is introduced in the *Edinburgh Review* by the following sentence:

"To enable our readers to judge of M. Anquetil's performance, we insert his version of the preface of the Prince Dara Shecuh, giving an account of

Voyage dans les Departemens de la France (*Ibid.*, art. 10, pp. 91-92), where internal evidence is of no avail.

[50] Vol. I, no. 1, October 1802, art. 5, pp. 44-59. Attributed to Hamilton by *WIVP*.

[51] In: *Ed. Rev.*, vol. I, no. 1, October 1802, art. 4, pp. 26-43.

[52] *Ibid.*, no. 2, January 1803, art. 2, pp. 412-421.

[53] *WIVP* attributes both to Hamilton.

[54] 4, for the Year 1802, 1803, Account of Books, pp. 13-18.

[55] *Ibid.*, pp. 18-33.

[56] 5, for the Year 1803, 1804, Account of Books, pp. 30-33.

[57] P. 414.

the motives for undertaking the work; to which we will annex our own translation, from the Persic copy in our possession," [58]

the wording of the *Asiatic Annual Register* clearly suggests Hamilton's lack of appreciation for the Persian work:

"Of the Persic work we have in our possession a complete copy. . . We shall present our readers with an English translation of this preface from the original, both as it explains the motives which induced the royal author to undertake the work, and as it is the only part of it which they could peruse with any sort of interest, or from which they could derive the smallest information." [59]

In both reviews we find Hamilton's idea that Aurangzeb published the work after his brother's death in order to justify his overthrowing him, and both reviews have the same identifications of Hindu deities with various Moslem entities. Both articles also condemn the complicated way in which Anquetil tried to give as literal a translation as possible of the Persian text; this point is stressed in the *Edinburgh Review* in a humorous vein:

"nothing less than the beatitude promised by Darah Shecuh, at the conclusion of his preface, to those who shall read and understand it, could induce any one to persevere in such an attempt, through the medium of M. Anquetil's version." [60]

Hamilton regrets that the *Oupnekhat* is but a Persian adaptation of an Upaniṣad and does not give the original text. In the *Edinburgh Review*, he expresses this opinion in a general way, understandable by the layman:

"We are of opinion, that a translation of an Upanisada, from the Sanscrit into English, would prove a performance of some interest; but that the value of the work before us is considerably diminished, by coming through the medium of a Persic translation." [61]

The corresponding passage of the *Asiatic Annual Register* is more technical; it recalls what is already known about the Vedas and concludes:

"A genuine abridgment of the Vedas, in the Sanscrit language, comprising the substance of all these particulars, would undoubtedly be a work of some value, and much curiosity; but the production of Darashucuh, neither furnishes any new facts on the subject, nor illustrates those which are already known." [62]

Both reviews cast doubts upon Anquetil's assertion that he knows Sanskrit; as could be expected, only the *Asiatic Annual Register* goes to the extent of giving some examples of Anquetil's errors:

[58] P. 415.
[59] P. 14.
[60] P. 421.
[61] P. 421.
[62] P. 16.

"It only remains to notice one thing more which not a little surprised us. The learned author informs the public, that he derived considerable assistance, in the execution of this laborious work, from his knowledge of the Sanscrit, of which he intends to publish a dictionary; yet, in almost every page, he betrays great ignorance of that language. We shall endeavour to shew, that the Sanscrit words, in his text, are only known to him through the medium of the Persic character. For instance, in the Devanagari alphabet, the sound of G and of K have each a distinct representation; whereas, in Persic, they are represented by the same character: hence GAVALGANI is written, KAPLKIANI; GARGA, KARK; GANDHARVA, KANAHERB; and so forth. In the next place, the short vowels are omitted in the Persic, but, in the Devanagari, they are distinctly represented: hence the RIK VEDA, is RAK, the JAGUR, DJIDJIR, &c. The diacritical points are frequently omitted: hence BUDYA, *knowledge,* is BADIA; VARUNA, the *Indian Neptune,* is BARAN. Numerous other examples might be adduced, but these we apprehend will be sufficient to prove that M. Anquetil has, at least, not availed himself of the knowledge which he professes to have of the Sanscrit language, in his version of the Upanisada." [63]

Anquetil's introduction to the *Oupnekhat* is not such as to give Hamilton a higher appreciation of the author's faculties than the one he had expressed in an earlier review of one of Anquetil's works. He says in the *Asiatic Annual Register*:

"But on these sublime topics of metaphysical theology, M. Anquetil does nothing more than bring together a variety of quotations from well known writers, which are not only often discordant, but which do not lead to any definite conclusion. His own observations are thinly interspersed; and only serve to shew, that the subject he labours to investigate, is altogether beyond his comprehension." [64]

At a time when the evaluation of things Oriental all too easily led to exaggerations, one must admire Hamilton's reaction in the *Edinburgh Review*:

". . . the venerable translator, who seems too readily to adopt the common error of considering every thing that is oriental as curious, every thing that is antient as sublime, and every thing that is mysterious as profound . . ." [65]

In his reviews of the sixth volume of the *Asiatick Researches,* both for the *Edinburgh Review* and the *Asiatic Annual Register,* Hamilton goes into a detailed analysis and criticism of three articles only: *On the Religion and Literature of the Burmans* by Francis Buchanan, *On Mount Caucasus* by Francis Wilford, and *On the Antiquity of the Surya Siddhanta* by J. Bentley.

As was the case in the reviews of Anquetil's *Oupnekhat,* the review of

[63] Pp. 17-18. [64] P. 17. [65] P. 413.

Buchanan's article in the *Asiatic Annual Register* is much more severe than the one in the *Edinburgh Review.* The latter article thus expresses Hamilton's objections to Buchanan's contribution—and reiterates his diffidence towards Paulinus—:

"As we shall find it necessary to object, in many instances, to the information furnished by this gentleman, and, in most, to dissent from his conclusions, it is proper to account, in some measure, for the confidence with which we venture to contradict a writer, whose opportunities of information on the subject he treats of, are peculiar to himself, and the other gentlemen of the mission. Dr Buchanan does not pretend to any acquaintance with the learned languages of the East; and he regrets, that his stay in the Burman dominions was too short to enable him to acquire theirs. In this predicament, his information is derived from a Romish missionary, and his etymological inferences from Paulinus. That Paulinus was unacquainted with the Sanscrit language, of which he has published a dictionary, it seems paradoxical to assert. It is nevertheless true, that, in his travels, he betrays a complete ignorance of that language, and quotes books for facts that are not to be found in them. His Sanscrit dictionary (which we have in vain endeavoured to procure) is, we will venture to assert, a dictionary of the Malabar idiom, which bears the same relation to the Sanscrit that Italian does to Latin, or the vernacular dialect of modern Athens to the language of Aristotle and Plato." [66]

The wording in the *Asiatic Annual Register* is much more direct:

"But unfortunately for the public, and still more for himself, instead of employing his time exclusively during his residence in the Burman empire, in examining its natural productions, he chiefly devoted his attention to the study of the vernacular language, the religion, and literature of its inhabitants. These objects are indeed of infinite importance; but they were not likely to receive much elucidation from Doctor Buchanan, who himself informs us, 'that he is totally unacquainted with the learned languages of Asia, and that he remained too short a period amongst the Burmans to acquire any knowledge of the idiom in which their books are composed.' Nevertheless he has thought his inquiries respecting their religion and literature of sufficient value to present the result of them to an Asiatic society. And in order to enliven the tediousness of his dissertation, and to entertain, since he could not instruct his readers, he has advanced various hypotheses, that are at least calculated to attract notice from their novelty, and from the confidence with which they are urged, if not to gain converts by the ingenuity and speciousness of the arguments by which they are supported." [67]

[66] Vol. I, no. 1, October 1802, pp. 30-31.

[67] 4, for the Year 1802, 1803, Account of Books, p. 23.

Both articles develop several of Hamilton's favorite themes. He insists upon the antiquity, importance and high degree of civilization represented by Hinduism, and supports Hinduism's priority to Buddhism. He maintains the excellence of Hindu domination as compared to the Mohammedan governments which followed. Hamilton's high opinion of the learned brahmans often finds expression in his writings; he therefore cannot tolerate Buchanan's contempt for them. He says in the *Asiatic Annual Register*:

"As to the epithets of *crafty Brahman, cunning Brahman, mean Brahman, cheating Brahman,* &c. &c. which our author so profusely bestows, they are suitable enough to the idle prating of a youth on his first arrival in India, but are utterly unworthy of a grave doctor, who aims at a place amongst the investigators of Asiatic history and science."[68]

In both articles, he opposes the view that Brahmanism might have been imported from Egypt. Thus in the *Asiatic Annual Register*:

"The striking affinity between the mythological systems of the Hindus and Egyptians, and the mention made in the Scanda-Puran of Nila, a sacred river in Cusha-Dwip, induced sir William Jones to hint at the probability of those systems having had a common origin. The learned and ingenious Mr. Wilford has endeavoured to prove, that the *Misra* of the Purans is actually Egypt; and upon this he has founded his celebrated hypothesis of the emigration from Hindustan to that country, which he supports with much ingenuity, and very uncommon learning; but the result of the vast mass of evidence which he has adduced, proves nothing more than that the ancient Hindus had some knowledge of the countries situated on the banks of the Nile. Doctor Buchanan, in a bolder spirit of conjecture, not only ventures to maintain the converse of Mr. Wilford's theory, but attempts to fix the aera of the introduction of the Brahminical religion into Hindustan."[69]

The two articles also illustrate his particular interest in ancient Indian geography. Here, as in numerous other works, he shows a great knowledge of Greek and Latin geographical sources; he quotes from such authors as Arrian, Pliny, Diodorus Siculus, Justin, and Plutarch. Of course, he also makes ample use of Indian and Persian works; in both articles, one finds, for instance, identical translations of the same passages of Abu'l Fazl, with only minor stylistic differences. More important, however, is Hamilton's reaction to one of three Burman tracts of which Buchanan has inserted a translation in his article. He writes in the *Edinburgh Review*:

"Our attention was powerfully arrested by the first of these, entitled, Cosmographia Burmana; but our astonishment was extreme, to discover this

[68] P. 29.

[69] P. 24.

supposed Burman document, to be a singularly mutilated and imperfect transcript, intermixed with the translator's observations, of a Sanscrit poem. The latter is named Khetra Nirmana, or the division of countries, and is unquestionably the most antient geographical tract now extant. It abounds in fable; but its extravagancies are compensated by the beauty of the imagery, and the harmony of the verse. The Burman version has retained only the fictions, and omits the names and descriptions of several hundreds of countries, mountains, and rivers, specified in the original." [70]

In the *Asiatic Annual Register,* he mentions the article of the *Edinburgh Review,* which he, however, attributes to a friend of his:

> "But the Cosmographia Burmana may excite some curiosity, from the resemblance which it bears to an episode in the Mahabharit, entitled the Khetra Nermana. We have been forestalled on this point, by a learned friend of ours in the Edinburgh Review, who has we think succeeded in shewing that the Burman Cosmography, as it is called, is a mutilated transcript of a Sanscrit poem." [71]

To prove their point, both articles give an extract from the Burman treatise with a translation of the corresponding passages in the Sanskrit text. Extract and translation are exactly identical, word for word.

In the *Asiatic Annual Register* the review of the *Asiatick Researches* is interrupted; the article by Wilford *On Mount Caucasus* is dealt with in the following volume. Whereas up to now the reviews in the *Asiatic Annual Register* were longer than the corresponding ones in the *Edinburgh Review,* this time the review of Wilford's article is much shorter in the former periodical than in the latter.

We have already had occasion to mention that Hamilton feels sceptical about Wilford's work. This is true with regard to the present article—and it will not change in the later reviews of articles by Wilford published in the *Asiatick Researches*—. His opinion is thus expressed in the *Edinburgh Review*:

> "His subsequent communications exhibit the same powers of combination, the same erudition and ingenuity, but usually suggest much wilder hypotheses; so that, whilst we admire the talents of the writer, we seldom feel disposed to acquiesce in his conclusions. In this class we must rank his supposition that the sacred isles of the Puránás, are those of Great Britain and Ireland; an hypothesis which would require the strongest proofs; and has hitherto been supported only by the weakest. The paper before us is distinguished by the same excellencies, and by similar defects: it abounds in assertions destitute of proof, and in valuable, judicious, and curious remarks." [72]

[70] P. 31. [71] P. 30. [72] P. 40.

He especially objects to Wilford because his analogies are based on words only, whereas the natures of the elements brought together are totally dissimilar. The tone is very much the same in the *Asiatic Annual Register*:

"Such are some of the principal hypothesis which captain Wilford, with his usual boldness has ventured to propose, and with his usual ingenuity and learning has strove to support. But we must confess that they appear to us extremely unsatisfactory: they establish no one historical or geographical fact; nor indeed do they furnish any information whatever, on which we can safely rely."[73]

The article of Bentley *On the Antiquity of the Surya Siddhanta* is dealt with in detail in the *Edinburgh Review* only. Hamilton endeavors to refute the opinion according to which the Sūryasiddhānta and consequently other Sanskrit texts which allude to it, date from a very recent time:

"His discussion relative to the antiquity of the Surya Siddhanta, involves points of the utmost importance; no less, indeed, than whether the whole of Sanscrit literature shall be considered as the spurious productions of a recent age, or genuine monuments of primeval times. We shall endeavour to do justice to his formidable attack on the Indian Gymnosophists."[74]

The review in the *Asiatic Annual Register*, although along the same lines, is extremely brief, so brief that we shall quote it here completely:

"The Surya Siddhanta, according to the received opinion in Hindustan, and to the positive assertion of the Pundits, is, the most celebrated as well as the most ancient astronomical work, of which the Hindu can boast. They universally believe it to have been received by divine revelation, 2,264,899 years ago.

"This calculation, which proceeds from the extravagant notions of time, entertained by the nations of India, merits not any investigation whatever; but every one conversant with Hindu astronomy, has allowed it to be a work of very high antiquity. In opposition to all this, Mr. Bentley has, in the paper before us, attempted to prove, by calculation, that the Surya Siddhanta, is entirely a modern production.

"It was our intention to have given, in this volume of our Register, a detailed reply to Mr. Bentley's apparently formidable attack on the antiquity of the Hindu system: but as it is not yet finally prepared, and as it is essential to be correct, even to a figure, we must unavoidably postpone it until our next Register. In the mean time, however, we will venture to affirm, that

[73] 5, for the Year 1803, 1804, Account of Books, p. 32.
[74] P. 42.

the data on which Mr. Bentley grounds his calculation, is erroneous, and that all his results, therefore, are widely distant from the truth." [75]

One looks in vain for the announced criticism of Bentley's paper in the subsequent issues of the *Asiatic Annual Register*, nor does one find a review of Pinkerton's *Modern Geography* which Hamilton had promised in his review of the sixth volume of the *Asiatick Researches.*[76] In fact, Hamilton's contributions to the *Asiatic Annual Register* had come to an end.

There may be an allusion to the termination of Hamilton's activities in the preface to the sixth volume of the *Asiatic Annual Register*, for the Year 1804, but published only in 1806. The editor, Lawrence Dundas Campbell, writes, on February 15, 1806:

"I now deliver to the public the Sixth Volume of the Asiatic Annual Register, which Work I originally planned, and have solely conducted. The motives which have hitherto induced me to conceal, and which now determine me to publish my name are merely personal, and therefore too immaterial to be mentioned. But it may somewhat lessen that dissatisfaction which the irregular publication of the Work has occasioned, to know, that it has been compiled and written, in the midst of the most distressing difficulties, from my own sources of information, and by my own labour, with inconsiderable assistance from the contributions of correspondants, and with no other encouragement than the barren commendation of the public. With a just sense, however, of that commendation, I have persevered in my undertaking, and have made every practicable exertion to support it.

"This explanation may likewise serve to shew in a more pardonable light, any deficiencies which may be found in this particular volume: it has been composed under an aggravation of those difficulties to which I have presumed to allude; and it certainly is inadequate to my own wishes. The Historical and Critical Departments are not sufficiently extended; partly owing to these causes, and partly to the voluminous collection of State Papers, which it was indespensable to insert." [77]

At the same time there is also a break in Hamilton's contributions to the *Edinburgh Review.* The reason for this cessation of all activities is a simple one: Hamilton had left England for Paris.

INTENDED PUBLICATION OF A GEOGRAPHICAL DICTIONARY OF ASIA

Before turning to Hamilton's stay in Paris, we must mention the fact that at the time he intended to publish a Geographical Dictionary of Asia, in

[75] P. 33.
[76] In: *Asiatic Annual Register* 4, for the Year 1802, 1803, Account of Books, p. 29, n.
[77] Pp. V-VI.

collaboration with Lawrence Dundas Campbell, the editor of the *Asiatic Annual Register.*

The fourth volume of the *Asiatic Annual Register* has the following announcement:

"*In the Press, and Speedily will be Published,*

In one large Volume, Octavo, Illustrated with a GENERAL MAP of ASIA, and with MAPS of HINDUSTAN, the Eastern ARCHIPELAGO, CHINA and JAPAN, TARTARY, the TURKISH DOMINIONS in ASIA, PERSIA, and ARABIA, from the most Authentic Materials; Engraved under the Direction of Mr. ARROWSMITH,

A GEOGRAPHICAL DICTIONARY OF ASIA.

CONTAINING

Concise but Particular Accounts of the EMPIRES, KINGDOMS, PRINCIPALITIES, PROVINCES, DISTRICTS, CITIES, TOWNS, FORTS, MOUNTAINS, PROMONTORIES, SEAS, HARBOURS, RIVERS, LAKES, &c.; together with Sketches of the Manners, Customs, and Institutions, of the various People who inhabit the Countries comprised in that Portion of the Globe.

The Information respecting HINDUSTAN and the Western Countries of ASIA, will be principally derived from SANSCRIT, PERSIC, and ARABIC MANUSCRIPTS; and the Accounts of the other Countries will be drawn, both from Original Sources, and from a careful Collation of the most Authentic European Geographers and Travellers, Ancient and Modern.

By ALEXANDER HAMILTON, Esq.

AND

LAWRENCE DUNDAS CAMPBELL, Esq.

Printed for T. CADELL and W. DAVIES, Strand; and J. DEBRETT, Piccadilly."[78]

An enterprise of this sort naturally is connected with Hamilton's special interest in ancient Indian geography, as is evidenced in his contemporaneous articles. As a matter of fact, the preparation of this Geographical Dictionary of Asia went back to a few years earlier. Indeed, two years before, the second volume of the *Asiatic Annual Register* already announced such a work to be published in the near future, but without mentioning the names of the scholars who prepared it. Here is the text of the earlier announcement:

"THE ASIATIC GAZETTEER.

In the Press, and speedily will be published, in one large volume Octavo, illustrated with Maps,

[78] For the Year 1802, 1803, Account of Books, p. 43.

A Geographical and Historical Dictionary
For Asia,

Containing

Concise but particular Accounts of the Empires, Kingdoms, Principalities, Provinces, Cities, Towns, Forts, Mountains, Promontories, Seas, Harbours, Rivers, Lakes, &c; together with Historical Sketches of the Manners, Customs and Civil Institutions of the various Countries comprised in that portion of the Globe.

The whole derived from a careful collation of the most authentic Asiatic and European Geographers, Historians, and Travellers; aided by the liberal Communications of Gentlemen who have been many years employed in the Honourable Company's Service in India, and who are conversant with Oriental Literature and Topography." [79]

Notwithstanding both announcements the book was never published. We have looked in vain through the sales catalogues of Cadell and Davies kept at the British Museum. Moreover, the authorship of such a work could not have escaped the attention of the authors of the articles about Hamilton in the biographical dictionaries. As far as we are concerned, we acknowledge that it was by mere accident that we came across the announcement of it in the *Asiatic Annual Register.*

The reasons why the book never came out are unknown. Admittedly, Hamilton left for Paris about that time; but he could have resumed his researches on the subject after his return to Great Britain if he had so desired.

We must mention here a problem for which we are unable to offer a solution, but which seems to us of some interest. If it is true that Alexander Hamilton never published his Geographical Dictionary of Asia or Asiatic Gazetteer, his brother Walter did publish, in London, in 1815, a work very similar, whose full title is: *The East India Gazetteer; containing Particular Descriptions of the Empires, Kingdoms, Principalities, Provinces, Cities, Towns, Districts, Fortresses, Harbours, Rivers, Lakes &c. of HINDOSTAN, and the Adjacent Countries, India beyond the Ganges, and the Eastern Archipelago; together with Sketches of the Manners, Customs, Institutions, Agriculture, Commerce, Manufactures, Revenues, Population, Castes, Religion, History, &c. of their various Inhabitants.*

The similarity in the titles of Alexander's announced work and of Walter's published book is striking. What relation there is, if any, between the two works, we have very little chance to find out. Anyway, L. D. Campbell having died in 1808,[80] the only person who could have made use of the notes of the

[79] For the Year 1800, 1801, Account of Books, p. 85.

[80] The 8th volume of the *Asiatic Annual Register*, for the Year 1806, 1809, was edited "by the late Lawrence Dundas Campbell."

still unpublished geographical dictionary was Alexander Hamilton. Whether he subsequently bestowed them upon his brother will probably remain unascertainable forever.

From what we have seen so far it appears that the years which Hamilton spent in Great Britain after his return from India were undoubtedly a very busy period; in the preceding pages we collected ample evidence of his productivity in the field of Oriental studies. It would not be necessary to add anything to what has already been said about this period of Hamilton's life, had not J. G. Alger declared that Hamilton went on a voyage to Constantinople. He says: "Alexander Hamilton, a future F. R. S., had been in the East India Company's service in Bengal, and, returning to England, after accompanying Lord Elgin to Constantinople, had continued his Sanscrit studies."[81] We cannot possibly agree with this statement. Lord Elgin's departure for Constantinople took place in 1799, and he came back through France just at the time of the rupture of the Peace of Amiens, in May 1803. This exactly corresponds to the period during which Hamilton published the articles which have been analyzed, and which prove that he stayed in Great Britain all those years. Alger's notice most certainly must be explained as the result of a confusion of Alexander Hamilton with William Richard Hamilton, who was private secretary to Lord Elgin and accompanied him on his expedition, a result of which was the famous collection of the Elgin marbles.[82]

[81] *Napoleon's British Visitors and Captives*, p. 89.

[82] Cf. A. H. Smith: *Lord Elgin and his Collection*, in: *Journal of Hellenic Studies* 36, London, 1916, pp. 163-372; see, *e. g.*, p. 168.

CHAPTER IV

PARIS: THE INTRODUCTION OF SANSKRIT ON THE CONTINENT

DEPARTURE FOR PARIS

The Peace of Amiens, signed on March 25, 1802, made it possible again to travel from Great Britain to France, and numerous British citizens availed themselves of this opportunity. Hamilton was one of them.

The exact date of Hamilton's departure to France is unknown, but it certainly took place after May 1802 and before April 1803. The *terminus post quem* is established by a letter from Jeffrey to Morehead on May 24, 1802, wherein Jeffrey complains about the prospect of the disintegration of the Edinburgh group, and wherein he mentions that "Hamilton spends his life abroad as soon as his father's death sets him at liberty."[1] The *terminus ante quem* is indicated in a letter of Francis Jeffrey dated April 1, 1803, which attests Hamilton's presence in France; we shall come back to this later.

The reason for Hamilton's voyage was, of course, related to his Sanskrit studies. Langlès, the keeper of the Oriental manuscripts in the National—formerly Royal, soon afterwards Imperial, and later on again Royal—Library in Paris, confirms it in the following terms: "Toujours occupé d'accroître les précieuses et vastes connaissances qu'il a déjà acquises dans la langue sacrée et la littérature des Hindoux, M. Alexandre Hamilton, profita des trop courts instans de paix qui rapprochèrent nos patries respectives, pour connoître et compulser les manuscrits en langue samskrite, que possède la Bibliothèque Impériale,"[2] and again: "M. Alexandre Hamilton . . . est venu exprès, à Paris, pour examiner et consulter la collection nombreuse et bien choisie de manuscrits samskrits et bengalis que possède la Bibliothèque du Roi."[3]

Although this French period lasted but for three or four years, it certainly is the most prominent one in Hamilton's life, the period also for which his name has become known to us. In order to understand this fact, we must remember that, at the time, *i.e.* the beginning of the romantic period, the intellectual elite on the European continent was anxious to have access to the Oriental languages and literature, but that, as far as Sanskrit was concerned,

[1] Cockburn: *Life of Lord Jeffrey*, vol. I, p. 138.

[2] Alexandre Hamilton-L. Langles: *Catalogue des manuscripts samskrits de la Bibliothèque Impériale, avec des notices du contenu de la plupart des ouvrages*, Paris, 1807, 118 pp., p. 7.

[3] *Notice de quelques ouvrages de littérature indienne; publiés au Bengale* (*suite*), in: *Mercure Etranger* 3, Paris, 1814, p. 155, n. 3.

they had not yet made any progress. The words of Sir William Jones's famous declaration were known and constantly repeated, but no one had the slightest knowledge of the wonderful language of India. The Asiatic Society in Calcutta and its publications, the *Asiatick Researches,* were considered to be the depository of all the knowledge in this respect. Now, all of a sudden, Paris was visited by a man who had been in India, who had learned Sanskrit besides other Oriental languages, and who did belong to the distinguished group of Sir William Jones's Asiatic Society. The response was immediate, and the intellectual and romantic elite assembled round such an eminent visitor. Moreover, here as in Edinburgh, Hamilton was soon appreciated for his friendliness and good character.

The best account of Hamilton's reception in Paris is by Langlès, the keeper of the oriental manuscripts, and one of those who most eagerly cultivated Hamilton's company: "il m'était recommandé par des amis communs; je l'accueillis avec l'empressement que devait m'inspirer sa réputation littéraire. Je ne tardai pas à reconnoître que les qualités de son coeur ne le cédoient pas à son mérite littéraire; nos fréquentes relations établirent entre nous, une amitié qui sera, j'espère, à l'épreuve du temps et des distances."[4]

PRISONER OF WAR

Hamilton had come to Paris after the Peace of Amiens had been concluded by France and Great Britain. But soon clouds obstructed the political horizon. In Edinburgh, Jeffrey expresses his anxiety in a letter to Francis Horner, dated April 1, 1803, which we already alluded to above: "Do you hear anything of Hamilton? I daresay these alarms will send him home, or at least the Sanscrit books, which are still more precious to him than his own person."[5] However, Hamilton stayed on in France, and he was affected by the decree of May 23, 1803, according to which all British subjects residing in Paris, who were within the age of 18 and 60 years, were to depart and assemble in Fontainebleau. In December of the same year, the British prisoners of war were transferred to Verdun and other fortresses.

The letters of Jeffrey show that he closely followed the development of the situation in France. In a letter to his brother John, dated July 2, 1803, he mentions "my excellent little Sanscrit Hamilton, who is also in the hands of Bonaparte at Fontainebleau."[6]

In reality there was no reason for Jeffrey to worry. If Hamilton ever went to Fontainebleau, as ordered in the decree, he certainly did not stay there long. He had influential friends who saw that he was not affected by the general measures.

[4] Hamilton-Langles: *op. cit.*, p. 7.
[5] Cockburn: *Life of Lord Jeffrey*, vol. II, p. 68.
[6] *Ibid.*, vol. II, p. 73.

In spite of a week of patient research in the National Archives in Paris, we have not been able to find any official document about him. Among the series of documents we consulted, two at least should normally have mentioned him. One is series F[7].2231-2258: "Etrangers de passage à Paris. An X–1814." In this series of registers in which were entered the names of foreigners of some importance who came to Paris, we hoped to find the exact date of Hamilton's arrival; it should be noted however that the information contained therein came from hotel managers and that some may have failed to give a complete list of their guests. The second series of documents which, we thought, would give us some information is series AF. IV. 1490-1498 "Bulletins de Police" from Messidor Year XII until December 1806. These reports were drafted by the Police Minister Fouché and were meant for Napoleon himself. They give minute details about the movements of British prisoners of war and about special permissions granted to them. However, we could find no mention of Hamilton, not even a trace of the permission he obtained to return home in 1806. This total absence of information leads us to the conclusion that Hamilton had a very special status and did not figure in the list of prisoners of war. The case is certainly not unique, but it remains somewhat exceptional nevertheless.

PRIVILEGED TREATMENT

One thing is sure: Hamilton was authorized to stay in Paris, and, as we shall see later, was allowed to live wherever he preferred. This fact is not surprising as far as the year 1803 is concerned: several distinguished British subjects were allowed to stay in Paris instead of being detained at Fontainebleau. But it becomes very surprising later on: in December 1803, the measures against British prisoners of war became strictly applied, so that almost all British males were assembled and kept under strict control in Verdun.

Hamilton's freedom of movement was such that, during the captivity of all others at Verdun, he could live in the house of a foreigner: Friedrich Schlegel, as we shall see below. Even more astonishing is the fact that Hamilton seems to have been allowed to make a journey to Aachen around June 1804. Indeed, on June 8, 1804, Dorothea Schlegel, who had left Paris for Cologne, writes to Helmine von Hastfer—later to become Helmine von Chezy—who had remained behind in Paris: "—In Brüssel war ich einen ganzen Tag, sah die Gallerie, die Stadt, den Park, und das Theater; Brüssel ist nächst Dresden für mich die schönste Stadt, und verdient allein eine Reise.—Hamilton grüsst Dich sehr, er hat mit lebhaftem Antheil Nachrichten von Dir angehört. Achen liegt in einer herrlichen Gegend, könnt ich einige Monate lang die dortigen Bäder gebrauchen, ich glaube gar ich würde wieder gesund.—

Cölln. . . ."[7] We quote this passage rather extensively, because we personally are in doubt whether or not we may infer from it that Hamilton went to Aachen; he may have been in Brussels as well. It is only the division marked in the text of the letter which, in our opinion, points to Aachen. Moreover, it may be supposed that Hamilton succeeded in going there for reasons of health, namely to take the well known baths.

Anyhow, from what we have already said above—and it will become even more evident from all we shall have to say about his stay in Paris—one can judge how misleading is the picture of Hamilton's life in Paris drawn by Rawlinson, both in *India in European Literature and Thought*: "One of the Company's servants, Alexander Hamilton, was detained in Paris during the Napoleonic wars. He spent his time in teaching his fellow prisoners Sanskrit, and among his pupils was the German poet and philosopher Schlegel,"[8] and in *Indian Influence on the West*: "Meanwhile one of the East India Company's servants named Alexander Hamilton happened to be in Paris in 1802, when hostilities broke out between Napoleon and the English,[9] and was detained there for three years. He spent his time in instructing some of his fellow-prisoners in Sanskrit."[10]

The privileged treatment which Hamilton enjoyed must have required the intervention of some very influential person. Chambers-Norman suppose that Langlès was this person.[11] However, we may doubt that Langlès was influential enough to obtain such a favor. In fact, Hamilton's protector was no less than the eminent Senator Volney, one of those who had smoothed the path for the First Consul, and was therefore entitled to his gratitude. This intervention is confirmed by Lanjuinais, one of Volney's friends and colleagues in the Senate: "M. Hamilton se livrait avec une vive satisfaction à l'examen de ces manuscrits, lorsque des ordres donnés à l'occasion du renouvellement de la guerre, le forcèrent à une prolongation de séjour en cette ville. Il profita de cette circonstance et des égards distingués que notre gouvernment voulut bien lui accorder, à la sollicitation du sénateur Volney, membre de la Société de Calcutta. . . ."[12] We even know of a letter written on Fructidor 5, Year XII, by Volney to Fouché, in which he recommends Hamilton to the minister. This letter, mentioned in J. Gaulmier's biography of Volney,[13] is briefly

[7] Ernst Wieneke: *Caroline und Dorothea Schlegel in Briefen*, Weimar, 1914, p. 367.

[8] P. 31. It should be remembered that, at the time, only British subjects were under restriction; Schlegel never was a prisoner. Moreover, Hamilton does not seem to have had any British pupils in Paris.

[9] The rupture of the Peace of Amiens took place in May 1803, not in 1802.

[10] P. 546.

[11] *Op. cit.*, p. 460.

[12] J.-D. Lanjuinais: *Mémoire sur la langue sanscrite*, in: *Oeuvres*, Paris, 1832, vol. IV, pp. 5-92, p. 55.

[13] Jean Gaulmier: *L'idéologue Volney 1757-1820. Contribution à l'Histoire de l'Orientalisme en France*, Beyrouth, 1951, pp. 484-485.

described by Charavay: "Il recommande à Fouché l'orientaliste Alexandre Hamilton."[14] Where the actual letter is preserved at present, we do not know, and Volney's biographer, Dr. J. Gaulmier, kindly let us know that he had no further information on the subject. Whatever the full text of this letter may be, it cannot have been Volney's first intervention in favor of Hamilton: in Fructidor Year XII Hamilton had already enjoyed more than a year of privileged treatment.

It could well be that Volney's letter of Fructidor Year XII was an attempt to obtain permission for Hamilton to return to Great Britain. The time was favorable, and several distinguished British subjects such as Sir Elijah Impey and James Forbes[15] were granted special passports. This is what Jeffrey seemed to hope for Hamilton too, when he wrote to Brougham on August 5, 1804: "I have better hopes of young Hamilton."[16] Nevertheless, whatever the purpose of Volney's letter to Fouché may have been, the fact remains that Hamilton did not return to his country at that time.

CATALOGUE OF SANSKRIT MANUSCRIPTS IN THE NATIONAL LIBRARY

Hamilton had a powerful argument for obtaining the very special status he enjoyed; Helmine von Chezy states it in these terms: "Alexander Hamilton, ein edler Schotte, der als Kriegsgefangener in Paris wohnen durfte, weil er sich erboten, die indischen Manuscripte, die Frucht der Siege des republikanischen Kriegsheeres, zu ordnen, und in ein Verzeichnis zu bringen. . . ."[17] Although we cannot fully agree with H. von Chezy as to the origin of the said manuscripts, we think that, as far as Hamilton himself is concerned, she was once again well informed. Considering the lively interest that Napoleon always took in Oriental studies, one is not surprised that Volney—the author of the *Voyage en Egypte et en Syrie* which was in high esteem especially after the Egyptian campaign—could arrange that a fellow Orientalist—the only one who knew Sanskrit on the continent at the time—should make a catalogue of the rich collection of Indian manuscripts in the National Library. Hamilton completed his task before returning to his country. Authors who have worked on the subject of the British prisoners of war in France during the Napoleonic wars have drawn the conclusion that it is to this

[14] *Fichier Charavay* preserved in the National Library in Paris, tome 176.

[15] Elijah Barwell IMPEY: *Memoirs of Sir Elijah Impey*, London, 1846, pp. 400-401; James FORBES: *Letters from France, written in the years 1803 & 1804*, 2 vol., London, 1806, vol. II, pp. 312-313.

[16] Henry BROUGHAM: *Life and Times of Henry Lord Brougham*, 3 vol., London, 1871, vol. I, p. 268.

[17] *Ueberlieferungen und Umrisse aus den Tagen Napoleons*, in: *Freihafen* III, 4, 1840, pp. 85-86.

catalogue that Hamilton owed his release,[18] and this seems fairly probable indeed.

Although Langlès puts it in a more elegant way, his testimony really amounts to the same: "La passion de l'étude et l'intérêt des matériaux qu'il avoit sous les yeux, retinrent M. Hamilton bien au-delà du terme qu'il avait fixé pour son voyage. Un évènement politique le força en outre, de différer son départ; il profita de la prorogation de son séjour à Paris et des facilités que lui accorda, en faveur de son rare mérite, un gouvernement protecteur déclaré des sciences et des savans, d'abord pour rectifier le Catalogue des manuscrits samskrits de la Bibliothèque Impériale. Les erreurs qu'il trouvoit à chaque article, le déterminèrent bientôt à refaire ce Catalogue. Il le composa en anglais." [19] The catalogue was published in French in 1807, after Hamilton had left Paris, jointly under the names of Hamilton and Langlès.

Some scholars have been very severe with Langlès in connection with the *Catalogue*. Adelung, for instance, bluntly says: "Der eigentliche Verfasser ist *Hamilton*; *Langlès,* der nicht im Stande war, nur das *Devanagari*-Alphabet zu lesen, hat nur dessen englische Handschrift übersetzt." [20] It is perfectly true, of course, that Langlès did not deserve to be regarded as a scholar, and that his works usually give no more than second hand materials. As far as the authorship of the *Catalogue* is concerned, one must admit that Hamilton and Langlès were not on the same level, but it must be remarked that Langlès never pretended anything else. In the preface, from which we gave extracts above, he describes his own contribution in the following terms: "Je l'ai traduit en français, et j'ai ajouté des notices plus ou moins étendues à un grand nombre d'articles. Quelques-unes de ces notices m'ont été fournies par M. Hamilton lui-même, j'ai tiré les autres des *Recherches Asiatiques,* de mes propres *notes* sur la traduction française des deux premiers volumes de ce savant recueil, des *Oeuvres* de M. Jones, du *Digeste des loix Hindoues,* traduit en anglais, par M. Colebrooke, des ouvrages du P. Paulin de Saint-Barthelemy et de différents manuscrits orientaux de la Bibliothèque Impériale." [21] Langlès's role in the *Catalogue* does not markedly differ from his usual type of publications: they are mostly translations into French from English originals enriched with notes added by Langlès himself from various sources. Moreover, Hamilton's biographer cannot but feel grateful to Langlès, if only for the reason that it is due to him that we possess the only book which ever bore Alexander Hamilton's name; and, considering the habits of the two men, we

[18] J. G. ALGER: *Englishmen in the French Revolution,* London, 1889, p. 265; and: *Napoleon's British Visitors and Captives 1801-1815,* p. 226; Michael LEWIS: *Napoleon and his British Captives,* London, [1962], p. 183.

[19] HAMILTON-LANGLES: *op. cit.,* pp. 7-8.

[20] *Bibliotheca Sanscrita. Literatur der Sanskrit-Sprache,* St Petersburg, 1837, p. 103, n.

[21] HAMILTON-LANGLES: *op. cit.,* p. 8.

can be sure that it was Langlès who decided that the catalogue should be published. Hamilton would no doubt have been satisfied to leave his autograph catalogue for private use in the Imperial Library.

There are two versions of the French printed catalogue: it first appeared in volume 4 of the *Magasin Encyclopédique* of 1807[22] and was afterwards published as a separate volume.[23] As compared to the publication in the *Magasin Encyclopédique,* the separate volume contains additions by Langlès, which consist in a catalogue of 14 "manuscrits en langue et en caractères bengalis," a "Note de M. Langlès, Sur quelques langues anciennes de l'Inde," and an index.

We have also compared the printed French catalogue of the Sanskrit manuscripts with Hamilton's handwritten English catalogue which is preserved in the National Library in Paris:[24] Langlès's preface as quoted above correctly delineates the contributions of both authors. The large type in the printed catalogue gives the translation of Hamilton's handwritten notices—of which some details, however, have been left out—, whereas the small type corresponds with the notes which do not belong to the original catalogue but which were afterwards added by Hamilton and by Langlès. Some modifications, however, have been made in the catalogue itself. In the handwritten catalogue, marginal notes have been added to some of the manuscripts listed as manuscripts in Bengali characters—we could not be sure if it was by Hamilton or by some other hand—, which indicate that they are in fact written in Devanāgarī characters. In the printed French catalogue, these manuscripts are accordingly listed among the manuscripts in Devanāgarī characters. The numbers, however, have not been changed, so that we sometimes have a missing number, and, sometimes, the same number occurring twice. It should also be noted that the two French versions of the catalogue already give a supplement of Sanskrit manuscripts to Hamilton's catalogue.

A point on which Hamilton certainly was not consulted is the orthography of the French catalogue. Hamilton's orthography has been profoundly modi-

[22] Paris, pp. 5-48, and 241-287.

[23] HAMILTON-LANGLES: *op. cit.* All references to the catalogue are made according to the pagination of this separate volume.

[24] *Ms. nouv. acq. fr. 5440: Catalogue of Books in the Sanscrita Language,* (*in*) *Devanagari Characters, in the National Library of France* (fol. 1-3); *Catalogue of Books in the Sanscrita Language,* (*in*) *Bengal Characters, in the National Library of France* (fol. 3-9); plus some notes on fol. 10. For the history of the Sanskrit collection in Paris and its cataloguing, cf. Jean FILLIOZAT's Introduction to the most recent *Catalogue du Fonds Sanscrit* (*Bibliothèque Nationale. Département des manuscrits*), Paris, 1941. Some data about Hamilton's catalogue will be found on pp. VIII-IX. On two points, however, Filliozat is in error, and both errors derive from his source, LANJUINAIS: *op. cit.*, p. 55. Hamilton did not arrive in Paris the same year which saw Anquetil-Duperron's death, *i. e.* 1805. And at the time he came to Paris, he was not yet a professor at the East India College, in Hertford.

fied, in order to assure a better pronunciation by speakers of French. We doubt that Hamilton would have agreed with that change since, in his later writings, he insists on the necessity of adopting a uniform system of transliterating Sanskrit names, namely William Jones's. And on p. 1 of his handwritten catalogue, he makes the preliminary remark: "The Orthography corresponds with the method adopted by Sir William Jones."

Perhaps it should be noted that Hamilton's handwritten catalogue also evinces his particular interest in the Purāṇas. On p. 3 verso, we find the following note:

"After the vedas, the Puranas are considered the most sacred of the indian Books. They usually commence with an account of the Creation, et furnish a summary of the most remarkable events from that time, to the particular period they chiefly refer to. They comprise probably many valuable remains of ancient history, every where intermixed with legendary traditions, & mythological fables. All the Puranas are in verse, et many passages possess great poetical merit. The whole are supposed to be productions of Crisna Dwaipayana, or island born, surnamed Vyasa, from his having divided the vedas into four Books: But the number & voluminous nature of these compositions, sufficiently demonstrates that they are not the work of one man."

LANGLÈS

Some authors have thought that Langlès became one of Hamilton's students in Paris.[25] No such information, however, appears in any contemporary source. On the contrary, Silvestre de Sacy says that "Le conservateur, satisfait d'associer son nom à celui de M. Hamilton dans la publication de ce catalogue, ne songea point sans doute à acquérir lui-même, à l'aide de celui dont il mettait à profit les talents, la connaissance d'un idiome si important pour la direction qu'il avait donnée à ses propres travaux."[26] Moreover, Langlès was far too busy publishing books, calculated to attract the general reader's attention; he certainly did not have the time to engage in a pursuit to which he would have had to devote all his efforts. But he did appeal to Hamilton

[25] LEFMANN: *op. cit.*, p. 19: "Langlès, der doch einer der ersten in Frankreich durch Uebersetzung des Wilkinschen Hitopadeça, 1790, sein Interesse für Altindisch an den Tag gelegt, der die erste Gelegenheit wahrgenommen, die merkwürdige Sprache auch selbst zu lernen, und seinen Lehrer, eben jenen Alexander Hamilton auch bewegen, seine unfreiwillige Musse einem Katalog der Sanskrithandschriften zu widmen, die seit Jahr und Tag in der 'Bibliothek des Königs' zusammen gebracht war"; also p. 18 and Nachtrag, p. XXXIII; LEVI: *op. cit.*, p. 339: "Langlès qui avait appris de lui (= Hamilton) les premiers éléments de la grammaire, mais qui n'avait pas poussé plus loin"; FILLIOZAT: *op. cit.*, p. IX; SCHWAB: *op. cit.*, pp. 75, 340.

[26] *Notice historique sur la vie et les ouvrages de M. de Chézy*, in: *Mémoires de l'Institut Royal de France, Académie des Inscriptions et Belles-Lettres* 12, 1839, p. 454.

on numerous occasions. He certainly talked with Hamilton about the works which he prepared, or even showed him drafts of his publications, for several of his books contain notes given him by Hamilton. Langlès never fails to acknowledge his debt, and his gratitude is always expressed in warm and sympathetic words; there is more than respect for the scholar, there is a deep friendship for the man.

We have mentioned above passages from Langlès's writings which testify to these feelings. But we could cite many more, such as the following note which is added to the review of Walter Hamilton's *East India Gazetteer* cited above; in 1815, *i. e.* nine years after Alexander Hamilton had left Paris, it still shows how honored Langlès had been to publish with him the Catalogue of Sanskrit Manuscripts: "J'ai traduit ce catalogue en français, en ajoutant des extraits de quelques ouvrages, et l'ai publié en 1807, heureux d'avoir l'occasion de placer mon nom à la suite de celui d'un savant aussi recommandable par ses qualités morales que par sa vaste et rare érudition." [27]

The work of Langlès which embodies the greatest number of notes by Hamilton is, of course, his French adaptation of the first two volumes of the *Asiatick Researches,* which was published during Hamilton's stay in Paris. We shall not even try to cite here all the passages in question; let us take as an example a sentence like this: "Cette note m'a été communiquée par mon savant ami M. Alexandre Hamilton, membre de la Société de Calcutta." [28] The references to Hamilton's catalogue of manuscripts are innumerable; it should be stressed that, at this time, the French translation had not yet been published; these references are consequently made to the catalogue of which Hamilton was the sole author. We shall only mention here a passage where the reference to Hamilton's catalogue is more elaborate than in most other cases: "Ce Pourâna étant le premier des dix-huit poèmes qui portent ce titre, et le plus important, je ne puis résister au desir de communiquer au lecteur la traduction de la Table des chapitres, faite par mon ami M. Alexandre Hamilton, membre de la Société asiatique de Calcutta, dont j'ai déjà eu occasion de citer plusieurs fois le nom avec les éloges dus à sa vaste érudition orientale et à son extrême complaisance. Il a fait cette traduction immédiatement d'après le texte sanskrit, qui se trouve sous le n° 18 nouveau et 87 ancien des manuscrits indiens de la Bibliothèque nationale." [29]

It would be hazardous to analyze Hamilton's ideas from secondary sources such as the notices by Langlès. It should be observed, however, that numerous

[27] P. 11, n. 1.

[28] *Recherches asiatiques, ou Mémoires de la Société établie au Bengale pour faire des recherches sur l'histoire et les antiquités, les arts, les sciences et la littérature de l'Asie; traduits de l'Anglois par* A. Labaume. *Revus et augmentés de notes, pour la partie orientale, philologique et historique, par* M. Langles . . . , 2 vol., Paris, an XIV = 1805, vol. I, p. 79; cf. also pp. 81, 225, 244, 266, 281, 289, 292, 306, 417, 419, etc.

[29] *Ibid.*, vol. I, p. 228.

notes concern Hindu mythology, and comparisons with Greek and Roman deities. In this respect, Hamilton sometimes rejects Jones's identifications. It is interesting to see then that Langlès quotes Hamilton as an authority, and places the two scholars on the same level. Langlès's confidence in Hamilton's opinion is also well expressed in the following passage: "j'ai eu tort d'attribuer à un défaut d'organe chez les Malabars, la terminaison nasale am qu'ils donnent à la plupart des mots sanskrits: M. Alex. Hamilton attribue cette terminaison aux principes de la langue malabare, qui emprunte l'accusatif des noms sanskrits, à-peu-près comme l'italien emprunte l'ablatif des mots latins." [30]

In his *Voyage pittoresque de l'Inde,* also published in 1805, there are several notes which had been suggested to Langlès by "un estimable savant de la Société asiatique de Calcutta, M. Alexandre Hamilton, dont j'ai fait la connoissance pendant son séjour à Paris, et que je puis compter au nombre de mes meilleurs amis." [31]

Although the works of Langlès published after Hamilton had left Paris contain far fewer notices of that sort, the contact between the two men seems never to have ceased. Langlès's *Monuments anciens et modernes de l'Hindoustan,* published in 1821, contains a note by Hamilton.[32] Moreover, in a review of Adelung's anonymously published *Rapports entre la langue sanscrit et la langue russe,* in which Hamilton happened to be quoted among the Sanskrit scholars,[33] Langlès says: "Le même orientaliste, dont la complaisance et la douceur égalent sa vaste érudition, m'a communiqué d'excellentes observations, dont j'ai enrichi les additions que j'ai faites à la traduction française des deux premiers volumes de *Recherches Asiatiques,* ou *Mémoires de la Société établie au Bengale, etc.,* en citant celui à qui je les devois avec les éloges et les expressions de gratitude qui lui étaient dus. M. Alexandre Hamilton a bien voulu aussi, à ma prière, faire un examen des *Relations des Indes et de la Chine, par deux voyageurs Arabes qui y allèrent dans le neuvième siècle,*

[30] *Ibid.*, vol. I, p. 524.

[31] L. Langles: *Voyage pittoresque de l'Inde, fait dans les années 1780-1783; Par M. William HODGES, Traduit de l'anglais, et augmenté de Notes géographiques, historiques et politiques,* Paris, 2 vol., 1805, vol. II, p. 141; cf. also pp. 185, 195, 213.

[32] Paris, 2 vol., vol. I, p. 88.

[33] St Petersbourg, 1811. Cf. pp. 3-4: "A mesure que les savans Anglais, les *Iones*, les *Colebrooke*, les *Hamilton*, et avec eux les *Anquetil du Perron*, les *Langlès*, les *Silvestre de Sacy*, les *Schlegel* et d'autres osèrent léver le voile mistérieux qui couvrait jusqu'aux traits de la langue *Sanscrit*," and pp. 7-8: "Je profite en attendant des matériaux que la précieuse collection des *Recherches Asiatiques*, les travaux du *Père Bartholomée*, de Mss. *Anquetil du Perron*, *Langlès*, *Hamilton* et *Schlegel* nous fournissent, pour mettre ensemble tout ce que j'y trouve d'analogue à la langue Russe pour la concordance des mots dans leur prononciation comme dans leur signification." Adelung does not mention any work by Hamilton; we suppose he refers here to Hamilton's contribution to the works of Schlegel and Langlès.

traduit de l'arabe, par l'abbé Renaudot. Il a fait sur ces relations des notes et des observations très-importantes, dont je compte enrichir la nouvelle traduction que je prépare, et qui doit accompagner le texte original de cet ouvrage, qui est déjà imprimé sous format in-18 avec les plus beaux caractères arabes de l'Imprimerie Royale. Si cet opuscule, dont l'authenticité et l'existence même ont été contestées, peut avoir quelque prix aux yeux des Orientalistes, c'est aux notes de M. Hamilton qu'il le devra. Il me sera doux de lui avoir moi-même cette nouvelle obligation, et de pouvoir lui payer publiquement un nouveau tribut de l'estime qu'il a inspirée à tous ceux qui l'ont connu pendant son séjour à Paris."[34] However, the intended translation was never published, and the man who later published a translation of the book maintained that nothing of the kind was found in the papers left by Langlès.[35]

Langlès even seems to have played the role of an intermediary between Hamilton and certain French scholars, as is attested by Lanjuinais: "M. Langlès, qui a soigneusement étudié, comparé tous ces caractères, m'avait fait observer, d'après M. Al. Hamilton, que les formes les plus pures et les plus exactes du devanâgari, duquel dérivent toutes les écritures de l'Inde, sont celles qu'on trouve dans la relation de l'ambassade du major Symes au royaume d'Ava."[36]

Although not a real scholar, Langlès played an important role in the history of Oriental studies. His house, his private library, as well as his department in the National Library were places where all learned people living in Paris at the time assembled and discussed recent developments of scientific research. It is most probable that it was there too, that Hamilton met several members of the French elite who were to become his students.

FRIEDRICH SCHLEGEL

Hamilton's most famous student in Paris undoubtedly was Friedrich Schlegel. Where the two men met for the first time is not known; it could have been in Langlès's house, or in Langlès's department of Oriental manuscripts in the National Library. Schlegel had come to Paris with the intention of learning Oriental languages, since the richest collection of works in Oriental languages was preserved there. He began with the study of Persian, leaving Sanskrit for later. In a letter to his brother, dated January 15, 1803, he

[34] *Notice de quelques ouvrages de littérature indienne,* in: *Mercure Etranger* 3, 1814, p. 155, n. 3.

[35] *Relation des Voyages faits par les Arabes et les Persans dans l'Inde et à la Chine. Texte arabe imprimé en 1811 par les soins de feu LANGLES. Publié avec des corrections et additions et accompagné d'une traduction française et d'éclaircissements par* M. REINAUD, Paris, 1845, p. VI, n.

[36] *Op. cit.,* p. 44.

gave a very material reason for that: "Die Sprachlehre des gewöhnlichen Indischen habe ich gleichfalls schon; aber das Sanskrit werde ich erst im Frühjahr anfangen können. Denn es wird auf den Bibliotheken nicht eingeheizt."[37] Four months later, on May 15, 1803, he informed his brother that he had acquired some notion of Sanskrit, and at the same time he mentioned Hamilton's name: "Sonst ist mirs aber vortreflich ergangen. Denn vieles, vieles hab'ich erlernt. Nicht nur im Persischen Fortschritte gemacht, sondern endlich ist auch das grosse Ziel erreicht, das ich des Sanskrit gewiss bin. Ich werde binnen vier Monaten die Sakontala in der Urschrift lesen können, wenn ich gleich alsdann die Uebersetzung wohl auch noch brauchen werde. Ungeheure Anstrengung hat es erfordert, da eine grosse Complication und eine eigne Methode des Divinirens und der Mühe; da ich die Elemente ohne Elementar-Bücher erlernen musste. Zuletzt ist mir noch sehr zu Statten gekommen, dass ein Engländer Hamilton, der einzige in Europa ausser Wilkins der es weiss, und zwar sehr gründlich weiss, mir mit Rath wenigstens zu Hülfe kam."[38] Three months later, he again spoke about his progress in Sanskrit, and Hamilton was again mentioned; this time, Hamilton did more than merely give advice, he regularly helped Schlegel in his work: "Ich habe unausgesetzt im Sanskrit gearbeitet und nun schon einen recht festen Grund gewonnen. Ich habe nun wenigstens schon eine Hand hoch Manuscript was ich mir copirt, liegen. Jetzt bin ich bei dem 2ten Lexikon was ich mir copire. 3-4 Stunden Tags Sanskrit geschrieben, und noch 1 oder 2 Stunden es mit Hamilton wieder durchgearbeitet; und wenn ich dann Abends aufgelegt war, fand ich immer auch noch Arbeit von 2-3 Stunden genug."[39]

The best evocations of the atmosphere which presided over Schlegel's Sanskrit studies with reference to Hamilton, we owe to Helmine von Chezy, who—this was before her marriage with Chézy—lived in Schlegel's house. There are two versions on the same subject. The description given in her autobiography is well known: "Er gab Friedrich täglich drei Stunden lang Unterricht im Sanskrit. Die Freude, einen solchen Schüler zu haben, war seine Belohnung; denn Friedrich Schlegel begriff mit bewunderungswürdiger Leichtigkeit und belehrte seinen Meister von seiner Seite. Alexander Hamilton war so wenig wie Schlegel ein trockener Gelehrter. Was er von der Wissenschaft erlangte, ging in seine Seele, sein Gemüth und seine Phantasie über. Man könnte dieses mit Recht von allen Indianisten sagen./ Das Studium des Sanskrit bereichert, läutert und erhebt das ganze Wesen des Menschen, es bemächtigt sich seiner ganz und gar, lässt nichts anderm mehr Raum, von keinem andern wird es in sittlicher Hinsicht in seinen Wirkungen übertroffen."[40]

[37] O. WALZEL (ed.): *Friedrich Schlegels Briefe an seinen Bruder August Wilhelm*, Berlin, 1890, p. 507.

[38] *Ibid.*, p. 511.

[39] *Ibid.*, p. 516. The letter is dated August 14, 1803.

[40] *Unvergessenes*, vol. I, p. 270.

However, the same author offered a much more detailed description elsewhere, in which the personalities of Schlegel and Hamilton were far more sharply contrasted than in the preceding one: "Alexander Hamilton . . . wurde Fr. v. Schlegels Lehrer im Sanskrit, nachdem dieser schon Persisch bei A. L. v. Chezy gelernt und sich eifrig vorbereitenden Forschungen für das Studium des Indischen gewidmet hatte. Schlegel bezweckte hierbei noch hauptsächlich sich in Frankreich eine Laufbahn zu eröffnen. Alexander Hamilton gab ihm eine geraume Zeit hindurch täglich von zwei bis fünf Uhr Unterricht. Dieser ausgezeichnete Sprachforscher hatte seine Jugend in Ostindien zugebracht, war dort einheimisch, befreundet mit den trefflichsten Brahmanen, und dergestalt in die Mysterien der wunderherrlichsten und reichhaltigsten aller Sprachen der Welt eingedrungen, dass sie, die vor einer Reihe von Jahrhunderten in ihrer eignen Vollendung und Grösse erstarrt, für ihn wieder lebte. An der Einwirkung dieses Studiums auf Phantasie und Gemüth seines Jüngers hatte A. Hamilton keinen Antheil. Er war der tüchtigste Sprachforscher, der beharrlichste und ausbündigste Handschriftentzifferer, ein höchst verständiger Mann, eine wackre, schönbegabte, klare und ausgeruhte Natur . . ./ Hamiltons Streben, den Geist der Indier aufzufassen, ging hauptsächlich darauf hin, die Verwandtschaft ihrer Mythen und die ähnlichen Züge ihrer Gottheiten mit den Griechischen zu entdecken.[41] Schlegel begnügte sich nicht mit einer Einzelheit der Anschauung, er umfasste mit Inbrunst das Ganze, und wollte es durchdringen mit der vollsten und brennendsten Fülle seiner Kraft. So kunstfertig nun auch Hamilton das Sanskrit handhabte, so redlich bemüht er auch war, es Schlegel beizubringen, blieben noch immer Klippen und Dornen ohne Zahl, die die Erkenntnis erschwerten, indess zugleich die Fülle der Wahrnehmungen dieser neuen Welt ihn übertäubte und verheerende Funken in sein Innres schleuderte. Er sprach unaufhörlich von der Heiligkeit der Büsser mit der höchsten Bewundrung als von dem Gipfel menschlicher Grösse, Dorothea hörte stillschweigend zu, sie mochte darüber im Klaren sein, dass ihr Mann sie nicht nachahmen würde. Ich liess mir gleichfalls solche Angst nicht beikommen, und meine gewohnte Achtung für den Meister, so wie das Gefühl der Unzulänglichkeit meines Urtheils bewogen mich, mit jedem Einwurf zurück zu halten. Hamilton hielt diese Büsser für Aberwitzige, Heuchler und Gaukler, für verächtliche Werkzeuge der Finsterlinge unter den Brahmanen; doch er sprach erst später mit mir darüber, und ich war bei Fr. v. Schlegels begeisterten Erzählungen, die er nach der Stunde bei Hamilton herüberbrachte, meinem eignen Gefühl überlassen."[42] As against the romantic and mystic Schlegel, Hamilton thus appears to have held a much sounder and more scholarly point of view.

[41] A preoccupation which indeed continually inspired his writings, both before and after his stay in Paris.

[42] *Ueberlieferungen und Umrisse aus den Tagen Napoleons*, in: *Freihafen* III, 4, pp. 85-87.

Schlegel, at least, did not lack enthusiasm, as is also shown in this letter addressed to his friend Tieck: "So frohe Tage leben wir nicht, wie in Dresden; aber gelernt habe ich in dem Jahre so viel, dass ich 's zeitlebens nicht bereuen könnte, hier gewesen zu sein. Anfangs hat mich die Kunst und die Persische Sprache am meisten beschäftigt. Allein jetzt ist alles vom Sanskrit verdrängt. Hier ist eigentlich die Quelle aller Sprachen, aller Gedanken und Gedichte des menschlichen Geistes; alles, alles stammt aus Indien ohne Ausnahme. Ich habe über vieles eine ganz andre Ansicht und Einsicht bekommen, seit ich aus dieser Quelle schöpfen kann." [43]

The contacts between Schlegel and Hamilton developed constantly. After having first been Schlegel's adviser, and then later having helped him more effectively, a new element came to change the relationship of the two men: Hamilton went to live in Schlegel's house, at nr. 19, rue de Clichy.

It is not known exactly when Hamilton moved there, but it must have been some time during the summer of 1803. A letter written by Schlegel to Chézy during that summer attests to this: "Mon tres cher Monsieur, Vous ne scauriez pas Vous faire une idée combien nous sommes en peine d'avoir eu la nouvelle que Vous continuez toujours de ne pas vous porter bien./ La première semaine des Vacances nous esperions presque tous les jours de Vous voir; et çe n'étoit que depuis quelques jours que nous avons sçu, que Vous etiez indisposé. J'espere que c'est passé actuellement avec le retour du beau temps, et que vous pourrez bientot nous en donner des nouvelles Vous même. Nous aurions été Vous voir chez Vous, mais ce n'est que depuis peu que nous avons Votre adresse, et ne scachant rien de Vos nouvelles nous craignons d'ailleurs, de Vous incommoder./ Mon epouse et Helmina [44] Vous souhaitent la reconvalescence et la santé la plus parfaite; et nous reunissons nos Voeux pour Vous voir bientot chez nous. Vous y trouverez aussi Mr. Hamilton, qui est actuellement chez nous, et qui de même est très affligé de ne pas Vous avoir vu dupuis si longtemps." [45]

We are inclined to put Hamilton's arrival at rue de Clichy near the end of August or the beginning of September 1803. Schlegel announced the fact in a letter to his brother dated November 26, 1803: "Ich lebe jetzt hier recht angenehm—so angenehm als es in der Fremde sein kann. Seit mehren Monaten wohnt Hamilton, der mein Lehrer im Sanskrit war, bei mir; auch ist Hagemann, ein junger Hannoveraner, der nicht nur gut Griechisch und Arabisch weiss, sondern auch sehr viel und sehr gründlich Persisch, unser Hausgenosse. Ausserdem noch drei junge Köllner,[46] die ein Privatissimum bei mir hören.

[43] Karl von HOLTEI (ed.): *Briefe an Ludwig Tieck*, 4 vol., Breslau, 1864, vol. III, pp. 328-329. This letter is dated September 15, 1803.

[44] Chézy's future wife.

[45] Josef KOERNER (ed.): *Briefe von und an Friedrich und Dorothea Schlegel*, Berlin, 1926, p. 54.

[46] Sulpiz and Melchior Boisserée, and Johann Baptist Bertram.

So habe ich angenehme Gesellschaft im Hause." [47] If on November 26 Schlegel said that Hamilton had lived there for *several* months, we must suppose that he meant for 2 months at least. However, the preceding letter of Schlegel to his brother, quoted above, is dated August 14; Hamilton's move must, therefore, have been later than August 14, but we may suppose that it took place within a month or so after that date.

The Schlegels lived in a constant state of financial insecurity, and to increase their income, they attracted paying guests to their house. Dorothea expressed her satisfaction in a letter addressed to Simon Veit on October 15, 1803: "Ich war schon entschlossen, Paris zu verlassen, als auf einmal alles eine andre Wendung erhielt. Ich habe Pensionäre bekommen, die theils bei uns wohnen, theils blos den Tisch haben. Seit dieser Woche haben sich wieder drei junge Leute aus Köln bei uns engagirt zur ganzen Pension, Tisch, Wohnung, &c. Uebrigens lassen diese sich von Schlegel ein Privatissimum über Poesie und Philosophie lesen, das sie sehr gut bezahlen, es sind sehr reiche Leute. Nächst diesen haben wir einen reichen kriegsgefangenen Engländer und einen jungen Hannoveraner, die beide mit Schlegel die orientalischen Sprachen treiben; nächstdem noch eine junge Frau, eine Deutsche, die mir in der Haushaltung sehr nützlich ist. Unser Haus ist also so besetzt (beim Tische sind auch noch zwei junge Franzosen), dass ich nicht daran denken kann, jetzt weg zu gehen." [48] Friedrich Schlegel himself gave a parallel report six months later, where it appears that the income was less important than foreseen: "Wir leben diesen Winter ganz anders als den vorigen und viel angenehmer. Wir hatten uns im Herbst vollständig eingerichtet, so dass wir nun mehrere Pensionäre annehmen konnten. Es lebten in unserm Hause drei junge Köllner die ein Privatissimum über Litteratur bei mir hörten, das sie mir recht gut (mit 1200 livres) bezahlten; ein junger Hannoveraner, der als ein sehr ausgezeichneter Orientalist mir empfohlen war; ferner Hamilton, der Engländer durch dessen Mithülfe vorzüglich ich das Sanskrit erlernt. Doch der letzte ass nicht an unserm Tisch wie die ersten.—Sehr viel Vortheil haben wir nun wohl nicht bei dieser Sache gehabt, theils weil es diesen Winter um so sehr viel ist theurer geworden, und wir doch den anfänglich gesetzten Preiss nicht erhöhen wollten." [49] The impression created by all this is that Schlegel had no objection to accepting money from the Boisserées both for his lectures and their lodging, whereas he accepted money from Hamilton for

[47] WALZEL: *op. cit.*, p. 523.

[48] J. M. RAICH (ed.): *Dorothea v. Schlegel geb. Mendelssohn und deren Söhne Johannes und Philipp Veit*, 2 vol., Mainz, 1881, vol. I, pp. 116-117; Ernst WIENEKE: *Caroline und Dorothea Schlegel in Briefen*, p. 360.

[49] Josef KOERNER (ed.): *Krisenjahre der Frühromantik. Briefe aus dem Schlegelkreis*, 3 vol., vol. 1-2, Brünn etc., [1936-1937], 3rd vol., Bern, [1958], vol. 1, p. 72. This letter, written to Charlotte Ernst, is dated April 10, 1804.

his lodging, and left his lessons unpaid. But, according to Dorothea, they all were rich people!

Notwithstanding this, the house of the Schlegels was an attractive place indeed. Sulpiz Boisserée writes in his autobiography: "Wir kamen auf diesen Gedanken, weil Schlegel, der sich eigentlich wegen dem Studium des Sanskrit in Paris befand, nebenbei deutsche Vorträge über Literatur versucht hatte; auch bewohnte er in einer schönen, stillen Gegend der Stadt zwischen Hof und Garten mit einigen Bekannten ein Stockwerk, wo noch einige Zimmer unbesetzt waren," and also "von meinen Fenstern konnte ich einen grossen Theil der weithin ausgedehnten Stadt übersehen, denn unser Haus lag sehr hoch in der Strasse Clichy, es war ehemals das Hotel des mit Helvetius, Diderot und Mirabeau oft gennanten pfälzischen Baron Holbach, den man für den Verfasser des Système de la nature hält." [50]

The same source also gives a description of the guests residing in the house: "Die Hausgenossenschaft bei Schlegel bildete ausser dem grossen Kenner des Sanskrit, dem A. Hamilton, eine kleine deutsche Kolonie; dazu gehörte der zehnjährige Sohn der Frau Schlegel, Philipp Veit, ein junger Philologe Hagemann von Hannover, der auch Sanskrit studirte, wir drei Kölner Freunde und Frau von Hastfer von Berlin, welche mit Frau von Genlis nach Paris gekommen war und nun die französischen Miscellen bei Cotta in Tübingen herausgab. An der Tischgesellschaft nahmen neben uns gewöhnlich nur Hagemann und Frau von Hastfer theil." [51]

For details as to how the rooms were distributed among Schlegel's guests, we have to turn, once more, to Helmine von Chezy: "Auf ihren (= the Boisserées') Wunsch liess Dorothea einige Zimmer im Hause, die eben leer standen, für sie einrichten; der Hannoveraner Hagemann nahm ein andres, und dem verehrten Hamilton wurde Schlegels Salon abgetreten, sie beschränkten sich nun auf ein grosses Zimmer mit einer Art Alkoven und einem Kabinet, wo Friedrich zu arbeiten pflegte." [52]

The arrival of the Boisserées at rue de Clichy in October 1803 slowed down Friedrich Schlegel's Sanskrit studies, as is testified by Helmine von Chezy: "Seit Boisserées Ankunft wurde Schlegel nachlässig in seinem Studium des Sanskrit." [53] Moreover, at the end of April 1804, Schlegel left Paris in their company and settled in Cologne. This did not, however, prevent him from recollecting Hamilton's lessons. In a letter to his brother, dated July 21, 1804, we read: "diese (= the exact pronunciation of Persian) ist mir fremd, denn in Frankreich kennt man sie nicht, und Hamilton liest schon so viel Indisch

[50] 2 vol., Stuttgart, 1862, vol. I, p. 23.

[51] *Ibid.*, vol. I, p. 24.

[52] *Ueberlieferungen und Umrisse aus den Tagen Napoleons. 4. Friedrich und Dorothea von Schlegel und ihr Uebertritt zur katholischen Kirche*, in: *Freihafen* IV, 1, Altona, 1841, p. 190.

[53] *Ibid.*, p. 191.

mit mir, dass ich ihm nicht damit beschwerlich fallen konnte, da ich für ihn zuweit zurück war, als dass es ihm hätte Vergnügen machen können,"[54] a passage which particularly well illustrates Schlegel's debt to Hamilton. Similarly, in a letter written during the summer of 1804 to Professor Paulus, he mentions the Sanskrit lessons in Paris thus: "Was mich betrift, so hab'ich in Paris mich fast ausschliessend mit der Persischen und Indischen Sprache beschäftigt; eigentlich mit der letztern, denn das Persische hab'ich da ich vor 5/4 Jahren durch einen lange in Indien unter den Braminen gelebten Freund die so seltne Gelegenheit das Sanskrit zu lernen erhielt, für welche Litteratur die Pariser Bibl. ganz besonders reich ist, hab'ich das Persisch etwas mehr vernachlässigt."[55] And, in the same letter, he goes on to say that he will have to go back to Paris, in order to learn more Sanskrit: "Paris liegt mir so dünkt mich, noch ganz hart am Rücken, und so wenig ich es sonst liebe, so muss ich doch auch wirklich des Sanskrit wegen wieder hin, da man etwas so seltenes und wichtiges, einmal angefangen, nicht wieder liegen lassen darf."[56] He did return to Paris in November 1804, and stayed there until March 1805; unfortunately, he was ill most of that time. Moreover, it is obvious that Schlegel's enthusiasm for any subject was brief, and we can very well apply to his abandoning Sanskrit studies the sentence in which Gertrud Richert has expressed his abandoning Provençal studies for Sanskrit: "Friedrich Schlegel's Begeisterung war rasch aufgeflackert und rasch erloschen."[57]

After Schlegel had left Paris, Hamilton stayed on in his house; Schlegel says that he was still there during the summer of 1805, but, when his brother decided to go to Paris, during the spring of 1806, Friedrich did not know where August Wilhelm would be able to find Hamilton; he did not neglect, however, to request his brother to convey his greetings to him, and he did so in a particularly warm way: "Eigentlich weiss ich aber nicht, ob es rathsam ist, Dir noch andre Addressen zu geben, da Du nur eine Woche in Paris bleiben willst; denn da wirst Du keine Viertelstunde zu verliehren haben. Weil Du es aber ausdrücklich verlangst so lege ich wenigstens eine für die Bibliothek von Chezy bei, meinen Freund und Persischen Lehrmeister.—Hagemann und auch Hamilton wohnten vorigen Sommer rue Clichy N° 19. in meiner ehemaligen Behausung; ob sie noch da wohnen, weiss ich nicht; [Du] kannst von Chezy vollkommne Nachricht über sie erhalten. Siehst Du etwa Hamilton, so vergiss ja nicht, ihm recht viel freundschaftliches von mir und über mich zu sagen."[58] In the letter written to Chézy on the same day,

[54] KOERNER: *Krisenjahre der Frühromantik,* vol. I, p. 127.

[55] UNGER: *op. cit.,* p. 17.

[56] *Ibid.,* p. 18.

[57] *Die Anfänge der romanischen Philologie und die deutsche Romantik* (= *Beiträge zur Geschichte der Romanischen Sprachen und Literaturen,* 10), Halle, 1914, p. 15.

[58] KOERNER: *Krisenjahre der Frühromantik,* vol. I, p. 325. August Wilhelm did not meet Hamilton, as is proved by a letter of Friedrich dated July 15, 1817, which we

May 2, 1806, he asks: "Je Vous prie de le (=August Wilhelm) presenter à Mr. Langles et de lui donner des renseignements sur Mr. Hamilton, s'il est encore a Paris ou non," and in the *post scriptum* he adds: "Si Vous voyez Mr. Hamilton, je Vous prie de lui rappeller mon souvenir et de presenter mes respects a Mr. Langles." [59]

The main result of Friedrich Schlegel's Sanskrit studies was his widely known book: *Ueber die Sprache und Weisheit der Indier*, published in Heidelberg in 1808. In his preface, Schlegel pays a high tribute to Hamilton: "Die Kenntniss, die es mir davon zu erwerben gelang, verdanke ich vorzüglich der Freundschaft des Herrn Alexander Hamilton (Mitglied der Calcuttaischen Gesellschaft, und jetzt Professor der persischen und indischen Sprache in England) der mir seinen mündlichen Unterricht vom Frühjahr 1803-1804 schenkte." [60] Besides Hamilton's lessons, Schlegel mentions that he made use of a manuscript in the Imperial Library, but there again, Hamilton helped him: "Schreibefehler oder Versehen, welche bei der ersten Abfassung eines so weitläuftigen Werks selten ganz vermieden werden, sind wohl nur wenige darin; nach dem Wurzelwörterbuch zu urtheilen, welches Herr Alexander Hamilton in meiner Abschrift zu revidiren, und mir einige Fehler darin anzuzeigen die Güte hatte." [61]

In a letter accompanying the copy of his book which was sent to Heyne, he again speaks of Hamilton's lessons: "Erlauben Sie mir den Nahmen eines Ihrer ehemaligen Schüler in Ihrem Gedächtnis zu erneuern und das Beifolgende Werk / über die Sprache und Weisheit der Indier / Ihrer Aufmerksamkeit zu empfehlen. Es enthält die Resultate meiner seit dem Jahre 1803 auf der Pariser Bibliothek unter der Anleitung und nach dem mündlichen Unterricht des Herrn Alexander Hamilton gemachten Studien." [62]

Lanjuinais, in his dissertation on the development of Oriental studies, also records Hamilton's role in Schlegel's work: "Un autre littérateur allemand plus connu, M. Frédéric Schlegel, reçut dans le même temps, à Paris, de M. Hamilton des leçons de sanskrit, et mit si bien à profit l'enseignement de cet habile maître, qu'il s'est trouvé en état de publier, à Heidelberg, en 1808, un curieux essai sur les langues et la littérature des Indiens, ouvrage en allemand, qui, par des recherches intéressantes et des idées profondes, a excité l'attention du monde savant." [63]

This is not the proper place to discuss the contents of Schlegel's work.

shall come to later. Actually, Hamilton by then had returned to Great Britain, as will be seen in the following chapter.

[59] Koerner: *Briefe von und an Friedrich und Dorothea Schlegel*, p. 79.

[60] P. IV.

[61] P. VI.

[62] Koerner: *Briefe von und an Friedrich und Dorothea Schlegel*, p. 105. This letter is dated May 2, 1808.

[63] *Op. cit.*, p. 56.

Moreover, two excellent studies appeared recently which give information about this subject. Ursula (Struc-)Oppenberg examined the sources of Friedrich Schlegel's translations from Sanskrit texts[64] and is still pursuing her research in connection with the critical edition of Schlegel's works. A. Leslie Willson, on the other hand, studied the evolution of Friedrich Schlegel's image of India[65] and concluded that, starting from a romantic mythical image, Schlegel very slowly developed towards a disenchanted but also more scientific representation of India, the process being complete in his work *Ueber die Sprache und Weisheit der Indier.* Willson attributes this change to the fact that Schlegel now had direct access to the sources; we on our part would not hesitate to hold that Hamilton played an important role in this evolution. The fact is that many of Schlegel's more mature opinions about India as expressed in his book are in absolute agreement with opinions expressed by Hamilton long before. It would no doubt be a work of high interest to make a thorough comparison between Schlegel's work and Hamilton's writings, on a much larger scale than Chambers and Norman's article[66] with regard to comparative philology.

It would not be possible to overestimate the role played by Schlegel's book: it was the first volume about Sanskrit written in German, and it excited an immense interest. It is due to this book that Franz Bopp decided to go to Paris and, following Schlegel's example, to study Sanskrit intensively. Friedrich Schlegel's book, in spite of all its imperfections, was the spark which gave rise to comparative philology.

AUGUST WILHELM SCHLEGEL

Friedrich Schlegel's Sanskrit studies not only inaugurated comparative philology, but Indian studies in Germany as well. Following his younger brother's example, August Wilhelm Schlegel in his turn studied Sanskrit—much more thoroughly than Friedrich ever did—, and became the first professor of Sanskrit in Germany. Friedrich's book *Ueber die Sprache und Weisheit der Indier* is his only work in the field of oriental studies; August Wilhelm became an excellent editor of Sanskrit texts.

The fact that, later on, August Wilhelm became a much better Sanskrit scholar than his brother has been at the basis of a confusion touching Hamilton. Thus, the article "Orientalistes" of the *Encyclopédie Nouvelle,* by L. Dussieux, says that "Auguste-Guillaume de Schlegel, alors à Paris, étudia à

[64] *Quellenstudien zu Friedrich Schlegels Uebersetzungen aus dem Sanskrit* (= *Marburger Beiträge zur Germanistik,* 7), Marburg, 1965.

[65] *A Mythical Image: The ideal of India in German Romanticism,* Durham, N. C., 1964, pp. 199-220. Willson makes the erroneous statement that Hamilton was made prisoner in France "on his way home to England" after his stay in India (p. 210).

[66] *Op. cit.*

cette époque le sanskrit, guidé par son ami Hamilton."[67] And in J.-B. Galley's *Claude Fauriel,* there is the same confusion between the two brothers.[68]

Other authors erroneously believe that the Schlegels were both students of Hamilton; thus A. F. Ozanam says that Fauriel "reçut avec M. Chezy, avec MM. Schlegel, les premières leçons de M. Hamilton,"[69] and J.-D. Guigniaut writes about the same Fauriel: "En relation intime, de très bonne heure, avec les deux frères Schlegel et avec notre Chézy, il reçut comme eux, de la bouche du célèbre prisonnier anglais, M. Hamilton, les premières notions de cette langue sacrée de l'Inde, le sanscrit,"[70] whereas Rawlinson states that "Chézy and Hamilton were responsible for teaching the brothers Friedrich and August Wilhelm von Schlegel, who in turn imparted their knowledge to Germany."[71]

In fact, it was only much later that August Wilhelm Schlegel began to study Sanskrit. He himself writes in 1819: "Erst seit fünf Jahren habe ich angefangen, das Sanskrit zu erlernen, und nur unter mancherley Unterbrechungen darin fortfahren können."[72] Following his brother's example, he went to Paris, but Hamilton was no longer there. In Bopp's biography, Lefmann writes: "Dann hatte Schlegel als Schriftsteller, als Uebersetzer und Kritiker bereits bedeutendes geleistet und sich einen Namen erworben, als er 1814 dem Beispiele seines Bruders folgte und Sanskrit zu lernen anfieng. Sein Lehrmeister in Paris war nicht sowohl oder gar nichts de Chézy, der Mitschüler des jüngeren Schlegels bei Alex. Hamilton, als vielmehr ein jüngerer Mann, mit dem er nach seinem Ausdruck 'oft gemeinschaftlich gearbeitet.' Er hat auch den Namen desselben—Herr Bopp aus Aschaffenburg—zuerst öffentlichs bekannt gegeben. Das war, wie wir wissen, in den Heidelberger Jahrbüchern, 1815."[73] We even know, from a letter of Friedrich Schlegel to August Wilhelm, dated July 15, 1817, that the latter and Hamilton had not yet met at that moment: "er (= Hamilton) hat eben wegen dessen, was er darüber gehört (Mme de Staël's illness), gar nicht geglaubt, Deine Bekanntschaft machen zu konnen, was er sonst sehr gewünscht hätte, obschon er an 4 Wochen in Paris war."[74]

[67] Paris, 1842, vol. VII, p. 80.

[68] Saint-Etienne, 1909, p. 259.

[69] *M. Fauriel et son enseignement,* in: *Oeuvres complètes,* vol. VIII, Paris, 1855, pp. 99-100.

[70] *Notice historique sur la vie et les travaux de M. C. Fauriel, lue dans la séance publique annuelle de cette Académie le 9 août 1861,* in: *Mémoires de l'Institut National de France, Académie des Inscriptions et Belles-Lettres* 25, Paris, 1877, p. 237.

[71] *Indian Influence on the West,* p. 547.

[72] *Ueber den gegenwärtigen Zustand der Indischen Philologie. Geschrieben im Sommer 1819,* in: *Indische Bibliothek* 1, Bonn, 1820, pp. 7-8.

[73] *Op. cit.,* Nachtrag, pp. XLI-XLII.

[74] WALZEL: *op. cit.,* p. 568.

HAGEMANN

Of all those who became Hamilton's students, Friedrich Schlegel has been the only one actually to publish a book about Indian studies. There is little doubt, however, that Gottfried Hagemann—who stayed with the Schlegels at the same time as Hamilton, both remaining there even after Schlegel himself had left Paris, and who also studied Sanskrit, as seen above—, had he not died so prematurely, would also have put the result of his researches in writing. Unfortunately, Hagemann died early 1809, before he could attain prominence. We have only very little information about him, the main source being an extensive and moving obituary which appeared in the *Morgenblatt für gebildete Stände*.[75] The author of this obituary, who signs himself C. G., describes Hagemann's enthusiasm for Indian studies and comparative philology. He mentions Hamilton's role, although Hamilton's name itself is not quoted: "Bekanntlich hatte Hagemann sich schon frühe dem Studium der morgenländischen Sprachen gewidmet. Die zufällige Bekanntschaft mit einem Manne, welcher die heilige Sprache der Braminen (Sanskritsprache) verstand, führte ihn zu jener tiefsten, bisher noch wenig erforschten Quelle des Alterthums, wo sich mit Recht die wichtigsten Aufschlüsse über so viele, den menschlichen Geist unmittelbar angehende Dinge erwarten liessen." [76] As a result of these studies, Hagemann fostered the idea of going to India, and, to earn the necessary money for the voyage, became the preceptor of the children of the king of Naples. He died in Rome, where he had gone from Naples to collect the boxes containing his manuscripts and papers which after a long and eventful journey had finally arrived from France. The zeal and passion with which he seems to have worked create the impression of a very promising young scholar. This is also the opinion of a distinguished contemporary, Lanjuinais, who mentions that Hamilton taught Sanskrit "au jeune Hageman,[77] Hanovrien, qui alors parvint de lui-même à lire les manuscrits sanscrits en caractères talinga. M. Hageman se serait fait un nom dans la littérature indienne, si une mort prématurée n'eût trompé nos espérances." [78]

VOLNEY

Although, as seen above, Hamilton lived in Friedrich Schlegel's house, and even though he had Schlegel and Hagemann as his students, this does not mean that he lived exclusively in a German environment. He also associated with French scholars, and some of them became his students too.

[75] *Einige Nachrichten über Fr. Hagemann, hauptsächlich die letzte Zeit seines Lebens betreffend* (*Aus dem Briefe eines Reisenden aus Neapel vom 26 Mai 1809*), in: *Morgenblatt für gebildete Stände* 185, Tübingen, August 4, 1809, pp. 737-739.

[76] *Ibid.*, p. 737.

[77] This incorrect spelling appears also in FILLIOZAT: *op. cit.*, p. IX, who drew his materials from Lanjuinais.

[78] *Op. cit.*, p. 56.

Volney, the eminent senator and traveler, who intervened in his favor with minister Fouché, availed himself of Hamilton's presence to learn some rudiments of Sanskrit. His friend and colleague in the Senate, Lanjuinais, reports: "Pendant son séjour à Paris, M. Hamilton fit part de ses connaissances sur la littérature sanscrite à son confrère [79] le sénateur Volney." [80] Filliozat,[81] Schwab [82] and Volney's biographer Gaulmier [83] are aware of this fact. Moreover, two notes sent by Volney to Langlès confirm his interest in Indian manuscripts, at the very time when Hamilton was in Paris: "Paris; 8 Frimaire an 13 / J'ai reçu de Monsieur Langlès Conservateur des Manuscrits Orientaux de la Bibliothèque Nationale le manuscrit indien numero 31./ Volney. Sénateur," [84] and "24 frimaire an 13 / Le Sénateur Volney a l'honneur de saluer Monsieur Langlès, et de lui demander le numero CCIII du catalogue de Fourmont intitulé grammaire Talenga, pour lequel le présent billet servira de recepisse./ Volney." [85]

FAURIEL

Hamilton's most frequently mentioned French student undoubtedly is Claude Fauriel,[86] who became famous as a historian of literature, and particularly of Provençal literature. The memoirs devoted to him after his death in 1844 refer to his Sanskrit studies under Hamilton. Ozanam, for example, says: "C'était le moment où l'on commençait à parler de la langue sacrée des Indiens, d'un idiome savant, poétique, dont l'étude allait livrer à l'Europe les trésors d'une littérature immense et renouveler les merveilles de la renaissance des lettres grecques au seizième siècle. M. Fauriel n'eut donc plus de repos qu'il ne sût le sanscrit. Il ne recula pas devant les difficultés d'un travail incertain, presque sans règles et sans livres, sur des textes épineux, quand il était facile d'attendre que d'autres eussent défriché cette terre vierge. Il reçut avec M. Chezy, avec MM. Schlegel, les premières leçons de M. Hamilton, savant anglais, prisonnier en France, et chargé ensuite de classer les manuscrits indiens de la bibliothèque impériale." [87] On the same occasion, Sainte-Beuve writes: "L'étude du sanscrit l'avait de bonne heure tenté;

[79] In the Asiatic Society of Bengal, to which Volney had been elected.

[80] *Op. cit.*, pp. 55-56.

[81] *Op. cit.*, p. IX.

[82] *Op. cit.*, p. 75.

[83] *Op. cit.*, p. 485.

[84] Preserved in the National Library in Paris: *ms. fr. 12765 fol. 238.*

[85] *Ibid., fol. 239.*

[86] See, besides the passages quoted hereafter, LEFMANN: *op. cit.*, p. 18, and Nachtrag, p. XXXIII; *DNB, s.n.* Hamilton; CHAMBERS-NORMAN: *op. cit.*, p. 460; LEVI: *op. cit.*, p. 339; FILLIOZAT: *op. cit.*, p. IX; SCHWAB: *op. cit.*, pp. 40, 75; GAULMIER: *op. cit.*, p. 485.

[87] *Op. cit.*, pp. 99-100.

il s'y était appliqué l'un des premiers en France. M. Hamilton, Anglais qui avait longtemps résidé dans l'Inde, et que la rupture de la paix d'Amiens retenait prisonnier chez nous, était peut-être le seul homme alors sur le continent qui sût le sanscrit: il l'enseigna d'abord à M. de Chézy, à Frédéric Schlegel et à Fauriel lui-même. L'étude de l'arabe sous M. de Sacy n'en souffrait pas; Fauriel était arrivé à lire avec sûreté la poésie dans ces deux langues."[88] The article on Fauriel in the *BU* has the following passage: "Il apprit le sanscrit du seul homme qui alors (1803) le sût en France. C'était un Anglais, M. Hamilton, ayant longtemps habité l'Inde, et dont la brusque rupture du traité d'Amiens avait fait un de nos prisonniers de guerre," whereas the *NBG* mentions Fauriel in its article about Hamilton.

In his commemoration address for Fauriel before the Institut National de France, Guigniaut says: "En relation intime, de très-bonne heure, avec les deux frères Schlegel et avec notre Chézy, il reçut comme eux, de la bouche du célèbre prisonnier anglais, M. Hamilton, les premières notions de cette langue sacrée de l'Inde, le sanscrit, que personne en Europe ne savait encore, et qui, avec les trésors d'une immense littérature, d'un caractère entièrement nouveau parmi celles de l'Orient, recélait dans son sein fécond les racines et les formes des langues de notre Occident presque tout entier et les titres généalogiques de ses populations. On n'en était point encore à la découverte de ces merveilles; quelques hommes seulement, depuis William Jones, les avaient pressenties. M. Fauriel se contenta de jouir des richesses imprévues, des termes de comparaison si neufs et si instructifs qu'offrait à sa critique déjà si étendue l'inépuisable poésie de l'Inde; il s'abreuva largement à la source de ces épopées démesurées, dont lui seul peut-être, à ce moment, était en état, chez nous du moins, de comprendre la composition."[89]

In his turn, Fauriel's biographer, Galley, writes: "Par Anquetil Duperron et Jones, la Perse et l'Inde antiques étaient entrevues. Sur cette trace lumineuse, très séduit par *Sakountala,* en même temps que de Chézy, sous la direction d'Alexandre Hamilton, Fauriel pénétra dans les études sanscrites et apprit la vieille langue de l'Inde. J. Mohl rapporte l'ardeur de son étude:/ Ce n'est qu'en voyant les grammaires et les vocabulaires écrits de sa main, les nombreuses copies et les traductions qu'il a laissées qu'on peut se faire une idée de la persistance qu'il y a mise.[90] Dans son espérance, ces études devaient éclairer les origines grecques et latines: elles le conduisirent de bonne heure—on le verra—à la notion historique du groupement des langues indo-européennes dont le rameau slave, seul, ne lui était pas directement

[88] *M. Fauriel,* in: *Revue des Deux Mondes,* Paris, 1845, vol. 4, p. 677, and in: *Portraits contemporains,* vol. II, Paris, 1847, p. 542.

[89] *Op. cit.,* pp. 237-238.

[90] Preface to FAURIEL's posthumous book: *Dante et les origines de la langue et de la littérature italiennes,* Paris, 2 vol., 1854, vol. I, p. III.

connu,"[91] and he adds in a note: "On peut voir dans les papiers de Fauriel les nombreuses copies de textes sanscrits quelques-uns soulignés d'une traduction latine: plus de cinquante cahiers; beaucoup consacrés à des extraits du *Ramayana./* Les études de la langue ont laissé trace dans de nombreux essais de lexicologie sanscrite, listes de mots pour un vocabulaire, racines, grammaires, etc. De sa main, on voit des copies sur Wilkins: *The radicals of the Sanskrita language.—Collection of the Sanskrit words to be found in the grammar of this language./* Et l'histoire de l'Inde, son état présent, l'intéressaient à cause de la survivance de la langue et de la transformation des idées très antiques. A ce point qu'il a copié en six cahiers un travail dont j'ignore l'auteur intitulé: *Population de la partie de l'Indostan occupée par les Anglais. Calcutta, janvier 1797.*"[92]

We can only regret that Fauriel never published any work directly related to his Sanskrit studies. He was much the same as Hamilton: he was not interested in publishing books, but enjoyed discussing with friends the results of his enquiries. Anyhow, his interest in Oriental studies made him one of the group who founded the "Société asiatique" in Paris, and he exhibited his knowledge of Sanskrit in his occasional reviews, such as of Bopp's *Conjugationssystem*[93] and *Nalus*,[94] and of Schlegel's *Indische Bibliothek*.[95] Even more interesting perhaps is the fact that in his course of 1834 in the University of Paris, he displayed his knowledge of Sanskrit in his lectures on the Indo-European languages.[96] The most important document, however, remains the series of notices which he added to Hamilton's catalogue of the Sanskrit manuscripts in the National Library in Paris, and which are still preserved there.[97]

RAYNOUARD

Walzel, the editor of Friedrich Schlegel's letters to August Wilhelm, mentions another historian of Provençal literature as one of Hamilton's students: "Alexander Hamilton . . . war Lehrer . . . Franz Just. Maria Raynouard's (1761-1836; Klette Nr. 257), des franz. Literaturhistorikers u. vergl. Sprachforschers."[98] The only one who makes a similar reference is Josef Körner, who, speaking of Friedrich Schlegel and Raynouard, says: "bei einem gemein-

[91] *Op. cit.*, pp. 190-191; cf. also p. 259.

[92] *Ibid.*, p. 190, n. 3.

[93] In: *Archives philosophiques, politiques et littéraires* 4, Paris, 1818, pp. 290-319 (not signed).

[94] In: *Revue Encyclopédique* 5, Paris, 1820, pp. 537-545.

[95] In: *Journal Asiatique* 1, 1822, pp. 44-48.

[96] *Dante et les origines de la langue et de la littérature italiennes*, vol. II, pp. 30-78.

[97] *Ms. nouv. acq. fr. 5441, fol. 6-39: Notices de quelques manuscrits sanscrits par M. Fauriel.*

[98] *Op. cit.*, p. 184, n. 2.

schaftlichen Lehrer, dem Sanskritisten Alexander Hamilton, hatten sie sich kennen gelernt."[99] Körner's statement, however, is manifestly erroneous. The relative chronology of the references to Raynouard and Hamilton in Schlegel's letters to his brother shows that he was acquainted with Raynouard before he met Hamilton. Indeed, in the letter dated January 15, 1803, where, as quoted above, he says: "das Sanskrit werde ich erst im Frühjahr anfangen können," he has already developed a certain intimacy with Raynouard: "Sollte mans nicht zu Stande bringen können auf Subscription mit so viel Grammatik, Noten und Vocabularium als nothwendig eine tüchtige Masse provenzalischer Gedichte drucken zu lassen?—Ich könnte mich dazu vielleicht mit einem gebohrenen Provenzalen assoçiiren, der viel Liebhaberei dafür hat."[100] Moreover, the first letter in which he mentions Hamilton also contains the news of a break with Raynouard; in his letter dated May 15, 1803, quoted above, just after having spoken of Hamilton and his first steps in Sanskrit, he goes on: "—Ueber die provenzalischen Manuscripte habe ich Dir im 2ten Heft der Europa eine Nachricht zugeschrieben; die über die Sylbenmaasse soll gleich nachfolgen.—Herrlich wär'es wenn wir gemeinschaftlich etwas dafür unternehmen könnten; es versteht sich dass ich mit Ernst darauf sinnen werde, und nun alle Gedanken bei Seite setzte, wie ich sonst dachte mich dazu mit einem Provenzalen zu associiren. Diese Leute sind hier doch zu unbeholfen, wenn sie auch Liebhaberei haben, fliesst sie meist nicht aus der ächten Quelle."[101]

We are convinced, however, that not only is Körner's statement erroneous, but Walzel's note as well. We have been unable to find, in the various biographies of Raynouard we consulted, any mention of his having been one of Hamilton's students, or even of his having studied Sanskrit at all. Walzel's reference to a letter in Klette's catalogue led us to suppose that the document on which his note was based was to be found there. However, this proved not to be the case. The letter which bears number 257 in Klette's list[102] has been published by Gertrud Richert;[103] Raynouard writes to August Wilhelm Schlegel about Provençal literature, not about Sanskrit.

We must therefore conclude that there is no evidence of Raynouard's having ever learned Sanskrit with Hamilton. Walzel's remark which was accepted and amplified by Körner, may perhaps have resulted from a confusion with the other French historian of Provençal literature, namely: Fauriel.

[99] *François-Juste-Marie Raynouard,* in: *Germanisch-Romanische Monatsschrift* 5, Heidelberg, 1913, p. 461.

[100] WALZEL: *op. cit.*, p. 506.

[101] *Ibid.*, pp. 511-512.

[102] Anton KLETTE: *Verzeichniss der von A. W. v. Schlegel nachgelassenen Briefsammlung*, Bonn, 1868.

[103] *Op. cit.*, pp. 48-49.

CHÉZY

Some authors have ranked among Hamilton's students the man who later, in 1814, occupied the first regular chair of Sanskrit created on the Continent: Antoine-Léonard de Chézy.[104] We have, however, most decisive evidence against this assertion; in reality, Chézy learned Sanskrit by himself, after Hamilton had left Paris. In his inaugural lecture in the Collège de France, he himself described his first steps in the study of Sanskrit: "Mais, soit insouciance, soit manque de courage, aucun François n'avait encore répondu à cet appel de la science. Plus porté par goût à ce genre d'études, ou doué peut-être de plus de patience, j'entrepris de soulever le voile qui déroboit à nos regards ce sanctuaire mystérieux. A mesure que j'en déroulois un pli, que je voyois luire à mes yeux quelque trait de lumière, ma curiosité prenoit de nouvelles forces, et, semblable aux initiés qui ne parvenoient à approcher du Dieu, qu'après avoir été soumis aux plus rudes épreuves, j'eus le bonheur, après mille fatigues, de pénétrer dans le Temple auguste où sont consignées les connoissances d'un des peuples les plus anciennement civilisés du monde."[105] In the introduction to his edition-translation of Śakuntalā, he once again relates his very first Sanskrit studies, at the end of 1806, *i. e.* after Hamilton's departure for England.[106]

In fact, Chézy, who preferred an isolated life, studied Sanskrit in secret. His wife, Helmine, who, even after she had left him, always thought highly of him, writes in her autobiography: "Der Streit über das grössere Alterthum der Aegypter oder Indier war damals noch nicht angeregt, denn in Paris kannte nur Alexander Hamilton das Sanskrit. Indess Fr. W. Schlegel es mit seiner Hülfe muthig erfasste, aber nich eigentlich in die Tiefen der Geheimnisse der Sprache eindrang, hatte sich der junge Chézy ganz im Stillen derselben bemeistert, wollte aber nicht eher an das Licht, bis er sie ganz besass, und machte seine Mutter und mich nicht eher zu Vertrauten, bis er nicht mehr weit vom Gipfel der erklommenen Höhe stand. Auch seinem Freunde Sacy hatte er solange alles verschwiegen. Sein thatkräftiger Geist hatte eine neue Bahn ersehnt und gefunden. Schlegel, glücklicher als er, konnte eine edle Freundshand ergreifen, um sich leiten zu lassen, Chézy musste sich selbst begnügen."[107]

[104] OZANAM: *op. cit.*, p. 100; SAINTE-BEUVE: *op. cit.*, *ibid.*; *NBG*: *s. n.* Hamilton; GUIGNIAUT: *op. cit.*, p. 237; WALZEL: *op. cit.*, p. 184, n. 2; LEFMANN: *op. cit.*, p. 18, and Nachtrag, pp. XXXIII, XLI-XLII; GALLEY: *op. cit.*, pp. 190, 259.

[105] *Discours prononcé au collège royal de France, à l'ouverture du cours de langue et de littérature sanskrite, le lundi 16 janvier 1815*, Paris, 1815, p. 2.

[106] *La reconnaissance de Sacountala, drame sanscrit et pracrit de Calidasa, publié pour la première fois, en original, sur un manuscrit unique de la bibliothèque du Roi, accompagné d'une traduction française, de notes philologiques, critiques et littéraires, et suivi d'un appendice,* Paris, 1830.

[107] *Unvergessenes,* vol. I, pp. 278-279.

If Chézy learned Sanskrit all alone, it was however by his own choice. Like Schlegel, he could have asked Hamilton to give him advice and help. Helmine herself acknowledges this fact: "En 1803, Alexandre Hamilton, Membre de l'Académie de Calcutta, qui avait passé une partie de sa vie dans les Indes, obtint la permission de faire le Catalogue des Manuscrits Indiens de la Bibliothèque, travail immense, auquel M. Langlès ajouta son nom, et même plusieurs notes de son écriture. M. F. de Schlegel, alors à Paris, étudia à cette époque le Sanskrit, guidé par son généreux ami, M. Hamilton. Ce fut dans la conversation de ces deux Savans que M. de Chézy puisa les premières notions sur cette langue, que l'on peut considérer comme la clef des mystères du passé, et comme la porte d'une nouvelle carrière pour les progrès intellectuels de l'avenir./ M. de Chézy m'avait rencontré chez M. de Schlegel (*Voyez*, dans *le Dictionnaire des Hommes vivans*, l'article *Helmina de Chézy*). Il me parlait souvent dans ce temps-là de l'attrait que le Sanskrit avait pour lui, s'il eût pu l'étudier alors; mais il était trop timide pour s'adresser à M. Hamilton, qui d'ailleurs esperait partir pour son pays, et il manquait absolument de matériaux pour cette étude."[108]

His friend and former teacher Silvestre de Sacy also refers to the fact that Chézy left the opportunity unexploited: "Le désir de se livrer à l'étude de la langue des Vedas lui fut inspiré, suivant toute apparence, vers 1803, par les relations que ses fonctions à la bibliothèque nationale lui donnèrent avec un savant anglais, qui, marchant, comme les Colebrooke et les Wilkins, sur les traces de William Jones, avait acquis une connaissance approfondie de la langue sacrée des Brahmes. M. Hamilton, c'était le nom de ce savant, se rendant aux instances de M. Langlès, avait entrepris le catalogue raisonné des nombreux manuscrits sanscrits que renfermait le dépôt confié aux soins du savant français . . . l'employé, qui voyait dans la littérature indienne une nouvelle source de ces jouissances dont son esprit et son goût avaient toujours été avides, conçut dès lors le désir de surmonter toutes les difficultés, et de joindre l'étude de la langue sanscrite à celle des langues de l'Asie qu'il cultivait déjà avec tant de succès. Toutefois il n'osa pas se faire initier à cette connaissance en recourant à la complaisance de M. Hamilton, qui certes n'eût pas mieux demandé que de faire pour lui ce qu'il faisait pour un autre savant qui a rendu et rend encore de grands services à la littérature indienne. Ce ne fut même que plus tard, et seulement en 1806, qu'il commença à exécuter son projet, au moyen des faibles secours que lui offraient les ouvrages du père Paulin de Saint-Barthélémy, et de quelques esquisses de grammaire qu'il trouvait dans le dépôt auquel il était attaché. C'était pour ainsi dire à la dérobée et avec une sorte de mystère qu'il se livrait à cette étude, comme s'il eût été à Bénarès, et qu'il eût craint de soulever contre lui le fanatisme jaloux de la caste sacerdotale. Ce secret toutefois n'en fut pas longtemps

[108] *Notice sur la vie et les ouvrages de M. de Chézy*, Paris, 1834, pp. 5-6.

un pour celui qui lui consacre cette notice, et qui l'encouragea à persévérer dans sa généreuse entreprise."[109]

Another contemporary, Lanjuinais, equally speaks of Chézy's Sanskrit studies, even before he became professor of Sanskrit; but he mentions him apart from Hamilton's students whom he had enumerated immediately before: "Enfin, je dois dire que M. de Chézy, employé à la Bibliothèque Impériale de France, section des manuscrits, est parvenu à lire fort bien le sanscrit en caractère devanâgari et en caractère *grantha*, et même à traduire en français des textes sanscrits."[110] It should also be noted that Chézy did not participate in the catalogue of Sanskrit manuscripts which Hamilton composed; Filliozat, however, when rightly mentioning this fact, commits a slight anachronism: "Chézy qui, à cette époque, s'initiait seul au sanscrit dans la grammaire de Pons et devait en 1815 en inaugurer l'enseignement au Collège de France semble être resté, quoique employé au cabinet des manuscrits, à l'écart des travaux du catalogue";[111] it was after Hamilton's departure, at a moment when the catalogue was already composed, although not yet published, that Chézy began to study Sanskrit. And Rawlinson is guilty of another anachronism, when he says that Chézy already knew Sanskrit before Hamilton came to Paris: "this brought him (= Hamilton) into contact with A. L. de Chézy, the first Professor of Sanskrit at the Collège de France, who had taught himself unaided except for the help of English works and Duperron's manuscripts."[112]

It is undeniable that, although Chézy did not study Sanskrit with Hamilton,[113] it was due to the latter's influence and example that he decided to acquire a knowledge of this language himself. Apart from the references to this fact already mentioned above, we may also quote the article "Orientalistes," of the *Encyclopédie Nouvelle*, by L. Dussieux: "Les rapports d'amitié que Chézy entretenait avec le savant anglais ne furent pas sans influence sur ses études; mais malgré le départ d'Hamilton, et le manque absolu des travaux des Anglais de Calcutta, Chézy parvint à se rendre maître de la langue sanskrite."[114] The *NBG*, under the article "Chézy," also mentions "l'arrivée de M. A. Hamilton, membre de l'Académie de Calcutta, qui obtint en 1803 la permission d'examiner les manuscrits indiens, éveilla dans l'âme de Chézy la première idée d'étudier le sanscrit."

JEAN-LOUIS BURNOUF

Among those who would have been able to be Hamilton's students, Schwab also mentions the classical philologist Jean-Louis Burnouf, the father of the

[109] *Op. cit.*, pp. 454-455.
[110] *Op. cit.*, p. 56.
[111] *Op. cit.*, p. IX.
[112] *Indian Influence on the West*, pp. 546-547.
[113] See also Levi: *op. cit.*, p. 339; Schwab: *op. cit.*, p. 75.
[114] Vol. VII, p. 80.

famous French orientalist Eugène Burnouf.[115] It is perfectly true that J.-L. Burnouf studied Sanskrit, but his teacher was not Hamilton; in reality Burnouf, exactly like his son a few years later, was a student of Chézy's. His biographer Auguste Morel says: "M. Burnouf, l'esprit ouvert à tous les enseignements de la science, était devenu le disciple de Chézy, pour qui l'on venait de créer au Collège de France la chaire de sanscrit."[116]

HAMILTON'S ROLE IN PARIS

When one examines the sum total of what Hamilton's students in Paris offered to the world of learning, one would, at first, be tempted to say that they did not contribute much to the progress of Oriental studies: Fr. Schlegel published one book, Hagemann died a few years later, Fauriel and Volney never made any contribution to Sanskrit studies. Is this the only result of Hamilton's having brought the knowledge of Sanskrit to the Continent? In reality Hamilton's role was much more important than it appears from a mere enumeration of the works of his direct students. We have already mentioned the decisive role which Schlegel's only work on Indian studies played in Germany and in Europe as a whole; we shall not come back to that point. But, even in France, where Hamilton's teaching did not lead to any publication whatsoever, his visit nevertheless had important results. Not only was the rich collection of Sanskrit manuscripts now catalogued and made accessible to scholars interested in the field, but the way to further progress was now open, and the ground was prepared. For the first time, it had proved possible to acquire, in Europe, a knowledge of the revered language of ancient India. For the first time a man, who had been in India, who had worked with pandits, who had known William Jones and who belonged to the famous Asiatic Society, for the first time such a man had imparted his knowledge to westerners. Sanskrit and Indian culture had become a subject of discussion, in the Parisian salons and in the study rooms of the learned. To be sure, Langlès never knew Sanskrit, but he communicated to friends and visitors the reflections of the famous English orientalist. Chézy, Burnouf, August-Wilhelm Schlegel, and, later, Bopp, did not work with Hamilton in Paris, but it was his presence, or what they indirectly heard of him, which was at the basis of their desire in their turn to learn Sanskrit. Hamilton's most important contribution was not so much that of a teacher—only Schlegel would be worth mentioning in that case—as that of an initiator, a catalyzer of Indian studies in Europe. Through his conversation, and through the echoes which it produced, learned Europeans had discovered the Sanskrit language and the culture of India. In the introduction to his French translation of Bopp's *Vergleichende Grammatik*, Michel Bréal gives

[115] *Op. cit.*, p. 75.
[116] *Eloge de J.-L. Burnouf*, Caen, 1847, p. 30.

a good idea of the atmosphere around Hamilton at the time: "En ce qui concerne la littérature sanscrite, il s'était formé à Paris, depuis 1803, un petit groupe d'hommes distingués qui recueillait avec une curiosité intelligente les renseignements venant de l'Inde sur une matière si peu connue. Un membre de la Société de Calcutta, Alexandre Hamilton, fut le maître de cette colonie savante: retenu prisonnier de guerre après la rupture de la paix d'Amiens, il employa ses loisirs à passer en revue et à cataloguer la belle et riche collection des manuscrits sanscrits formée pour la Bibliothèque du roi, dans la première moitié du XVIIIe siècle, par le père Pons: en même temps, par ses conversations, il introduisait dans la connaissance du monde indien Langlès, le libéral conservateur des manuscrits orientaux, Frédéric Schlegel, Chézy, qui devait plus tard monter dans la première chaire de sanscrit fondée en Europe, et Fauriel, dont la curiosité universelle ne se contentait pas des littératures de l'Occident." [117]

Hamilton's influence upon his environment was of a purely personal character, and based on relations of individual with individual. Basham erroneously associates him with the Ecole des Langues Orientales Vivantes: "In 1795 the government of the French Republic founded the Ecole des Langues Orientales Vivantes, and there Alexander Hamilton (1762-1824), one of the founding members of the Asiatic Society of Bengal, held prisoner on parole in France at the end of the Peace of Amiens in 1803, became the first person to teach Sanskrit in Europe." [118] The fact is that Hamilton was totally independent of any institution; all the information he imparted about Indian languages and culture was in the context of his social, personal and friendly relations with the intellectual elite living in Paris at the time.

[117] François BOPP: *Grammaire comparée des langues indo-européennes. Traduite sur la deuxième édition et précédée d'une introduction par* Michel BRÉAL, Paris, 5 vol., 1866-1874, vol. I, p. XII.

[118] *Op. cit.*, p. 6.

CHAPTER V

EAST INDIA COLLEGE: TEACHING AND PUBLICATION OF CLASSBOOKS

RETURN TO GREAT BRITAIN

We have not been able to determine the exact date of Hamilton's departure from Paris, but it certainly took place in February or March 1806. No British subject would have been granted a passport for England without Napoleon's effective approval; and that could occur only during a period of relative peace between the two countries. Early in 1806, however, the circumstances were favorable: Napoleon had come back to Paris on January 26, after having defeated the third coalition. Great enthusiasm reigned after this successful campaign which culminated in the brilliant victory of Austerlitz. After January 26, and before Napoleon's departure against the fourth coalition in October of the same year, several British prisoners were granted various permissions. Consequently, on the French side, the only possible period for Hamilton's release is from February to September 1806.

The reference to 1807 as the year of Hamilton's release, given by Chambers-Norman,[1] and to 1808, by Michael Lewis,[2] must be erroneous. Hamilton resumed his contributions to the *Edinburgh Review* in the number for October 1806, as we shall see later. Moreover, on April 7, 1806, Charles Wilkins, the famous Sanskritist, then the librarian for the East India Company, recommended him for the Oriental professorship at the recently founded East India College. The *Minutes and Reports of Committee of College,* for April 9, 1806, record: "Another Letter from Mr Charles Wilkins dated the 7th Instant, being also read, recommending Mr C. Hamilton of the Bengal Establishment, as Oriental Professor at the College. Order'd that the same do lie for future Consideration."[3]

In spite of the error in the initial—a confusion which will continue and even become worse in later reports—, this document leads us to the conclusion that Hamilton was by then back in England, and that he had almost immediately visited his friend Wilkins.

[1] *Op. cit.,* p. 460.

[2] *Op. cit.,* p. 301.

[3] India Office Records J/2/1, p. 139. Unpublished Crown-copyright material in the India Office Library and the India Office Records transcribed in this book appears by permission of the Secretary of State for Commonwealth Affairs.

APPOINTMENT TO THE EAST INDIA COLLEGE

The recommendation by such an established Sanskrit scholar as Wilkins was decisive, and Hamilton obtained the post of Oriental professor in the East India College. The *Minutes and Reports of Committee of College* on August 6, 1806, give the following report of the deliberation: "The Committee having taken into consideration the appointment of a proper person as Oriental Professor to the East India College, in the room of Dr Jonathan Scott who on his resignation was succeeded pro tempore by Dr. J. B. Gilchrist, that the Committee being of opinion that two Professors in the Oriental Department, are necessary at the East India College, one to teach the Sanscrit and other Hindoo Languages, and the other to instruct the students in the Persian, Hindostanny etc. They accordingly beg leave to recommend to the Court that two Oriental Professors be appointed to the East India College./ And the Committee having maturely considered the Testimonials and Qualifications of the several Gentlemen, who are Candidates for the situation of Oriental Professor at the East India College viz./ Major Herbert Lloyd[4]/ Captain C. W. Hamilton (*corrected by a later hand into* Alexander Hamilton Esqr.)/ Captain Charles Stewart, and / Mr. H. G. Keene[5] / further beg leave to recommend to the Court that Captain C. W. Hamilton (*corrected to* Alexr Hamilton Esqr), and Captain Charles Stewart be appointed, Professors at the said College, the former of the Sanscrit and other Hindoo Languages and the latter of the Persian, Hindostanny etc., these Gentlemen appearing in every respect fully qualified for the above professorships./ The Committee also beg leave to recommend, that each of them have the same salary and advantages as Dr Scott possessed, viz. £500 per Annum and Apartments in the College, or House Rent in lieu thereof with his Commons the same to commence from their joining the College, and actually entering their respective duties."[6]

The same text appears in the *Proceedings of Court of Directors re E. I. College,* under the date August 27, 1806, where it was "resolved by the Ballot Unanimously."[7] In this report however the mention of "Capt. C. W. Hamilton" has not been corrected.

The incorrect title of Captain given to Hamilton in these reports has been perpetuated in the *Memorials of Old Haileybury College,* and, thence, in the *DIB.* Danvers writes: "Before the opening of the College Mr. Jonathan

[4] We have not been able to find any information about this gentleman. He is mentioned neither by the *DNB* nor by the *DIB,* and does not seem to have published any work.

[5] H. G. Keene senior, Hindustānī scholar; although not appointed at this stage, became an assistant to his successful rival Stewart later (cf. *Royal Kalendar for 1820,* London, p. 282).

[6] J/2/1, pp. 150-151.

[7] J/3/1, the pages are not numbered.

Scott tendered his resignation as Oriental Professor, whereupon Dr. John Gilchrist offered his services gratuitously until another Professor should be appointed, which offer was accepted. Dr. Gilchrist acted in that capacity from the 12th February to the 19th May, 1806,[8] and was succeeded by Captain Alexander Hamilton as Professor of Sanskrit, and Captain Charles Stewart as Professor of Hindi."[9] Monier-Williams, however, seems to have perceived a difficulty in this title of Captain, since he says that Hamilton "seems to have dropped his title of Captain."[10]

TEACHING

Hamilton thus became the first man to teach Sanskrit effectively and regularly in Europe.

The East India College, first established in Hertford Castle, and moved into the new buildings at Haileybury in 1809, was meant for the instruction of future civil servants of the East India Company. The students were youths, aged at admission from 16 to 19, all members of well-to-do families, who, through the patronage of one of the Directors of the East India Company, secured appointments in India, sure to afford them enviable careers. Although, under such circumstances, the school authorities were not in a position to keep them under strict discipline, the program at least constituted a serious effort to give them the rudiments of the kind of knowledge which would make them good administrators in India.

As far as Oriental languages were concerned, the requirements in the *Directions for the Guidance of the Students of the East India College*, 1814, *i. e.* at a time when Hamilton taught there, were as follows:

"IV—The Test required in the Oriental Languages.
The following are the Oriental Languages to which the attention of the Students is required; viz.
1. Students destined for the "Bengal Presidency"—to *Persian, Bengalese,* and *Hindoostany.*
2. Students for "Madras"—to *Sanscrit,* and the *Hindoostany* or the *Persian.*
3. Students for "Bombay"—to *Persian* and *Hindoostany.*
Students admitted in Jan. 1814, or in any subsequent Term, will not be permitted to leave College until they shall have obtained from the Oriental

[8] Although Gilchrist ceased to teach on May 19, 1806, Hamilton, as we have seen, was not appointed before August 1806. MONIER-WILLIAMS, on p. 201 of the same book, HODSON: *op. cit.*, and the *DIB* are wrong when they infer from Danvers's statement that Hamilton began his teaching as early as May 1806. WINDISCH: *op. cit.*, vol. I, p. 57, n. 2, on the other hand, erroneously places Hamilton's appointment in 1808.

[9] F. C. DANVERS, M. MONIER-WILLIAMS, etc.: *Memorials of Old Haileybury College*, Westminster, 1894, p. 16, n. 1.

[10] *Ibid.*, p. 202.

Professors and Oriental Visitor[11] a Certificate of their having attained a certain proficiency, ascertained by the following Test.
1. Writing the Character peculiar to each Language in a fair and legible hand.
2. A thorough acquaintance with the terms of Grammar, as used by the Persians and Hindoos.[12]
3. A competent knowledge of the rudiments of each Language.
4. Reading, translating, and parsing an easy passage in each of these Languages; and if Sanscrit be one, furnishing an analysis of it.
5. The difficulties attending the study of the Sanscrit Language do not render it advisable to oblige, indiscriminately, all those destined for the Madras Presidency to persevere in it, unless their capacity furnishes some prospect of their efforts being successful. They shall all, however, be required to commence it; and if, after a trial of two months, it shall not appear to the Sanscrit Professor expedient to continue it, in the case of individuals, they shall be required to direct their attention to Persic and Hindoostany.
6. The study of the Sanscrit is not expressly enjoined to the Students destined for Bengal and Bombay; but such as voluntarily undertake it will be understood to furnish a very favourable pledge of their zeal and assiduity in the Company's service." [13]

Hamilton's task at the East India College is not well defined in the official report cited above, according to which he is appointed professor "of the Sanscrit and other Hindoo Languages." However, since to the other professor appointed is allotted the teaching of "the Persian, Hindostanny etc.," and since, on the other hand, the Oriental languages taught at the College were, according to the program quoted above, Persian, Hindustani, Sanskrit and Bengali, only the teaching of Bengali remains unassigned. But we know from other sources that Bengali was also taught by Hamilton. This is apparent from the *Minutes and Reports of Committee of College* and from the *Proceedings of Court of Directors re E. I. College* which we shall come to later. Moreover, the daybook of the Library of the East India Company shows that 29 Bengali grammars and other works were sent to the East India College for Hamilton's classes.[14] The daybook also mentions that 28 Marathi grammars by Carey were sent to him,[15] which seems to indicate that, besides Sanskrit

[11] Charles Wilkins at the time.

[12] This led Hamilton to compose a work entitled *Terms of Sanskrit Grammar* in 1814, as will be seen later.

[13] *Extracted from the " Statutes and Regulations framed and enacted by the Authorities specified in the Act of Parliament 53 Geo. III. cap. 155."*, East India College, 1814, pp. 9-10.

[14] *Library Day Book 1801-1814*, on February 15, 1809; April 7, 19, and July 31, 1810.

[15] *Ibid.*, on February 15, 1809.

and Bengali, Hamilton also taught the rudiments of Marathi, even though this language does not figure among the Oriental languages cited by the *Directions for the Guidance of the Students of the East India College* quoted above.

The official title of Hamilton's function, which normally appeared after his name from now onward, is mentioned for the first time in the *Royal Kalendar for the Year 1808.* This volume gives the following account of the Oriental Department of the East India College, Established at Hertford, 1805: "*Professor of Arabic,*[16] *Persian, and Hindostanee,* Charles Stewart, esq./ *Professor of Hindû Literature, and of the History of Asia,* Alexander Hamilton, esq./ *Visitor in the Oriental Department,* Cha. Wilkins, esq., F.R.S. LLD."[17] It thus seems that, besides Oriental languages, it was also Hamilton who taught Indian culture and history.

The two Oriental professors combined their efforts in insisting upon the importance of Oriental languages and of Sanskrit especially. Lord Minto's address delivered at the College of Fort William on September 15, 1810[18] gave them an excellent opportunity. The *Minutes and Reports of Committee of College* for May 3, 1811, say: "Letters from professors Stewart and Hamilton, in the Oriental Department at the College, the former dated the 28 March last, addressed to Charles Grant Esq. and the latter to Dr Wilkins, visitor to the College in the Oriental Department and dated the 6th Ultimo, both containing Observations and Remarks upon Lord Minto's Speech, at the Disputation held at the College at Fort William 15,, September 1810; and the latter containing some suggestions in consequence being read./ It was/ Resolved that the cultivation of the Sanscrit Language by the Servants of the Company in India, is, as important to the interests of the Company, as it is beneficial to the Individual pursuing that study; and therefore / That Instructions ought to be sent to Bengal, that upon the arrival of a Writer in Calcutta, he should be required to prosecute the knowledge of the Sanscrit Language, previously obtained by him, at the Company's College in England."[19]

LIFE AT THE COLLEGE

As long as the College was located in Hertford Castle, Hamilton lived outside the precincts. In a letter to another member of the Jeffrey group, Murray, his Edinburgh friend Francis Horner gives a charming description of Hamilton's life at that period: "I went down on Saturday last with

[16] Another language which does not appear among those taught at the College cited by the *Directions for the Guidance of the Students.*

[17] P. 293.

[18] The text of Lord Minto's address is reproduced in the *Asiatic Annual Register* 12, for the Year 1810-1811, 1812, pp. 425-441; see especially pp. 434-437.

[19] J/2/1, pp. 123-124.

Whishaw to Hertford, on a visit to Malthus[20] and little Hamilton. The Pundit is very happy, and gets very fat; in two years' time, I take it, he will have a figure in which it will be hard to say which is length, and which breadth, and which thickness. In a little comfortless lodging, I found him with Sanscrit proof sheets of a grammar,[21] sitting in the most perfect content, and ready to discuss any proposition. He is very much liked, as he may well be, by every body, for his sense and his temper."[22]

When the College moved to the permanent buildings at Haileybury, Hamilton enquired whether he could be accommodated within the precincts. The *Minutes and Reports of Committee of College* for March 3, 1809, mention: "On reading a letter from professor Hamilton, dated the 3rd Ultimo, requesting to know whether any of the Houses at Hayleybury are destined for his reception, in order that he may give an Answer to the Landlord of his present House, as to his renewing his Lease thereof./ Resolved, that Mr Hamilton be informed, that he may accommodate himself, as to the renewal of the Lease of his House or not as may most suit his convenience; and that his present allowance of House Rent, will in either Case, be continued to him."[23] We shall see that, on his retirement, in 1818, he occupied one of the houses within the College.

We know, however, that he also had an apartment in London, for, on January 26, 1811, the daybook of the East India Library notes that Wilkins brought him a book "to his appartment in London."[24]

RESIGNATION FROM THE COLLEGE

At the beginning of the year 1818, Hamilton announced his desire to leave the College. The *Minutes and Reports of Committee of College* for January 9, 1818, mention: "A Letter from Professor Hamilton dated the same day was read intimating his earnest wish to retire as soon as possible from a situation the duties of which had become too arduous for him to execute to his own satisfaction at the same time expressing a hope that the manner in which he had discharged them for nearly twelve years would justify his expectations that the Court would not think him undeserving of their

[20] Malthus, the famous economist, also a Whig, was a colleague of Hamilton at the East India College, where he was "Professor of History and Political Economy"; cf. *The Royal Kalendar for the year 1808*, p. 293.

[21] Most probably pages of Wilkins's Sanskrit Grammar, which Hamilton reviewed in the 13th volume of the *Ed. Rev.*, in January 1809. Horner's letter is dated October 27, 1808; and the *Library Day Book 1801-1814* mentions, for October 21, 1808, that a copy of Wilkins's Grammar was sent to Hamilton (cf. also the account of Wilkins's Grammar on p. 33 of the transactions).

[22] L. Horner: *Memoirs and Correspondence of Francis Horner*, vol. I, p. 463.

[23] J/2/1, p. 327.

[24] *Library Day Book 1801-1814.*

favorable consideration observing that if with a view to subsequent arrangements it should be thought indispensable that he should remain at the College a short time longer he would undoubtedly sacrifice his own earnest wish to the desire of the Court but requesting that they would name some time after which his services would be dispensed with & their merits considered." [25]

Hamilton did remain in charge for one more term. On May 6, 1818, the *Proceedings of Court of Directors re E. I. College* report his definitive resignation: "A Letter from Alexr Hamilton Esq F. R. S. dated at Haileybury the 2nd Inst. tendering his resignation of the situation of Professor of Sanscrit & Bengalese at the college expressing his hope that his past services will meet favorable Consideration & requesting to be allowed to continue in the House which he now inhabits until the 1st July next, being read / Ordered That it be referred to the Committee of College to examine & report." [26] The Committee considered Hamilton's request on May 27; at that date the *Minutes and Reports of Committee of College* read: "In pursuance of a reference of Court of the 6th Inst. The Committee have taken into consideration a Letter from Professor Hamilton stating that he had remained at the College during the present Term in obedience to the wishes of the Court conveyed thro' the late Chairman and respectfully soliciting to resign his Office at the expiration of that period stating his hopes that his services during the last twelve Years will experience a favorable Consideration that the Court know too well how to appreciate the respective merits of their servants to render it necessary for him to enter on the indelicate task of stating the grounds on which those hopes are founded that he appeals to facts within the knowledge of all the Members of the Court and is convinced he may safely confide his case to the discriminating justice of the Court & further soliciting permission to continue to occupy the House he at present inhabits 'till the 1st July next./ And the Committee recommend to the Court that Mr Hamilton be permitted to resign his situation at the College at Midsummer next & to occupy the House he at present inhabits till the 1st July./ They further recommend that in Consideration of the services of Mr Hamilton during the period of nearly twelve years which he has been attached to the College viz. from Augt 1806 to the present time and his having conducted the Department commited to his charge in a manner highly beneficial to the students as well as honorable to himself that he be granted a Pension of £200 P. Ann. to commence at Midsummer next when his present salary and allowances will cease." [27]

On the same day, the same source also provides us with the decisions about Hamilton's replacement: "The Committee to the Court in consequence of the retirement of Mr. Hamilton that Mr. Haughton be appointed till the expiration of his Furlough to fill the vacancy in the Oriental Department

[25] J/2/3, pp. 91-92. [26] J/3/2, p. 212. [27] J/2/3, pp. 135-136.

occasioned by the resignation of Mr Hamilton with the Salary & Allowances enjoyed by that Gentleman." [28]

These two recommendations of the Committee were submitted on the same day to the Court of Directors. The *Proceedings of Court of Directors re E. I. College* report, under the date of May 27, 1818: "Two Reports from the Commee of College dated this day being read one recommending that professor Hamilton be permitted to retire on a pension of £200 P Ann. from Midsummer next and to occupy the House he at present inhabits 'till the 1st July the other submitting that Mr Haughton be appointed 'till the expiration of his Furlough to fill Mr Hamiltons Situation with the Allowances enjoyed by that Gentleman / Ordered That the said Reports lie a week for Consideration." [29] On June 3 the report was approved as far as Hamilton's retirement was concerned: "Resolved that Alexr Hamilton Esq one of the (Oriental *added by another hand*) Professors at the College be permitted to resign his situation at Midsummer next and to occupy the House he at present inhabits 'till the 1st July./ And that in consideration of the Services of Mr Hamilton during the period of nearly twelve years which he has been attached to the College he be granted a Pension of £200 P Ann. to commence at Midsummer next when his salary & Allowances will cease." [30]

The decision of the Court was immediately notified to Hamilton, who thanked the Court in a letter, which is mentioned in the *Proceedings of Court of Directors re E. I. College,* for June 10, 1818: "A Letter from A Hamilton Esq late Professor of Sanscrit at the East India College dated the 8th Inst. returning thanks for the pension of £200 P Ann. lately granted to him." [31]

Two days later, the Court decided to appoint Graves Chamney Haughton as Hamilton's successor: "A Report from the Commee of College dated the 27th Ult° which was read in Court on that day and then ordered to lie for Consideration being again read./ *Resolved by the Ballot* that Lt Graves Chammy (*sic*!) Haughton of the Bengal Establishment be appointed 'till the expiration of his Furlough to fill the vacancy in the Oriental Department at the College occasioned by the resignation of Mr Hamilton with the Salary and Allowances enjoyed by that Gentleman." [32] Graves Chamney Haughton, who had left the Bengal Army and come back to England for reasons of health, had been appointed assistant Oriental professor in 1817. He succeeded Hamilton as professor of Sanskrit and Bengali, and stayed at the East India College until 1827, having arranged in the meanwhile that his furlough should be transformed in a final resignation from the army. The articles "Haughton" in the *DNB* and *DIB* date Hamilton's retirement and Haughton's appointment in 1819, whereas the exact date, given by the documents cited

[28] *Ibid.*, p. 134.
[29] J/3/2, p. 213.
[30] *Ibid.*, p. 214.
[31] *Ibid.*, p. 215.
[32] *Ibid.*

above, is June, 1818. This confusion reproduces an error in the *Royal Kalendar for 1819*,[33] which continues exactly the same composition for the Oriental Department as in 1818, the modified situation appearing only for 1820.[34]

PUBLICATION OF CLASSBOOKS

Hamilton's position as Oriental professor at the East India College led him to write a number of works, all of which are devoted to Sanskrit. We have already seen that Hamilton did not have much interest in publishing books. The works we refer to here directly derive from the necessities of his teaching. They were not meant to be made public; they were printed at the East India Company Press for the use of students at the East India College only. However, contemporaneous scholars outside the College tried hard, and some succeeded in securing copies of Hamilton's classbooks.

The idea of printing books for the use of students came from Hamilton himself, as is shown by a passage of the *Minutes and Reports of Committee of College*, on January 18, 1809: "The Deputy Chairman read to the Committee an Extract of a Letter from A. Hamilton, Esq., Sanscrit professor at the College as to furnishing the College with various Class Books in the Sanscrit and other Oriental Languages, as therein described./ Ordered, that the Chairman and Deputy Chairman, be authorized to obtain an Estimate of printing the Books in question and that they be requested to lay the same before this Committee,/ That this Committee also agree to the reference, proposed by Mr. Hamilton, in the said letter, to be made to the Madras government." [35]

On July 20, 1810, the problem of procuring books for the teaching of Sanskrit and Bengali is again mentioned, but the Committee wants to restrict the expenses: "A seventh Report from the College Council dated the 10 May, being also read, transmitting a Letter from Professor Hamilton, relative to Books and Documents received, or still required from India, for the use of the Sanscrit and Bengal Classes./ And the Committee referring to the Bengal Letter in the Public Department, paragraph 47, recently received; by which it appears, that several of the works mentioned in Professor Hamilton's Letter are transmitted to England./ Resolved that all the works mentioned by Mr Hamilton do not appear to be necessary, but those only, which are elementary; that the Sanscrit press will very shortly be able to supply many of those which are requisite; and that an Indent will be framed for procuring those from India, which shall be found wanting." [36]

[33] P. 282.
[34] *Royal Kalendar for 1820*, p. 282.
[35] J/2/1, p. 318.
[36] *Ibid.*, p. 531.

EDITION OF THE HITOPADEŚA

The first of the works published at the East India Press, an edition of the Hitopadeśa, came out at the end of 1810.[37] It bears no signature. However, apart from the mention "Haileybury" at the end of it, the text of the advertisement itself unmistakably points to the professor of Sanskrit at the East India College as the editor: "The determination of the Court of Directors of the East India Company to impart to gentlemen destined to the civil service in India some knowledge of the ancient language of that country, by instituting a *Sanskrit* professorship at Haileybury College, involved the necessity of procuring an immediate supply of class books. The expence of printing books in Bengal, with the delay and uncertainty of obtaining them from thence, rendered it expedient to attempt the impression of *Sanskrit* works in England. The importance of the object, in facilitating the acquisition of all the vernacular derivatives throughout India, was abundantly obvious; but the difficulties which presented themselves rendered the possibility of carrying it into execution in this country far otherwise, and seemed to interpose an insurmountable obstacle to the intentions of the court. Those impediments have at last disappeared, and a press, already amply furnished with materials for printing, not only in this antient language, but in one of its most useful offsprings, the dialect peculiar to the Province of Bengal, has been established, and this, at present its only issue, is the first *Sankrit* book ever printed in Europe."[38] Once again Hamilton proves to be a pioneer in the field of Sanskrit studies: after having been the first teacher of Sanskrit on the Continent, after having held the first regular chair of Sanskrit in Europe, he now edits the first Sanskrit text in the West.

The fact that the book was printed in the Devanāgarī characters designed by Wilkins, the fact also that it contained an edition of the Hitopadeśa, of which Wilkins had published a translation earlier, induced H. Bernstein to believe that the book was the work of Wilkins.[39] There can be no doubt, however, that Hamilton was the editor. Besides the advertisement cited above, we have indisputable testimony of contemporaries, which we shall come to later. Moreover, the daybook of the library of the East India Company on several occasions mentions the name of Hamilton as related to the progress of the publication:[40] on June 7, 1809: "Sent to Professor Hamilton. Hertford./ 24 Copies of the second sheet of the Hitopadéṣa"; on January 11, 1810: "Sent to Professor Hamilton, Hayleybury / 1 Copy of 3 Sheet of the

[37] *The Hitōpadēsa in the Sanscrita Language*, London, Library, East India House: Cox, Son and Baylis, Printers, 1810, VIII-124 pp., 4º.

[38] P. V.

[39] *Sanskritische Literatur*, in: *Leipziger Literatur-Zeitung*, 291, Leipzig, November 11, 1820, col. 2323. Same error in LEFMANN: *op. cit.*, p. 64.

[40] *Library Day Book 1801-1814.*

Hitopadéṣa"; on January 30, 1810: "Sent to Professor Hamilton 20 Copies of the First three sheets of the Library Edition of the Sanskrita Hitopadesam taken hence by Mr H. in person." Whereas the preceding notices eventually might be considered as pertaining merely to Hamilton's teaching, on March 21, 1810, the reference is more explicit: "Sent to Mr Hamilton / Hitopadesa 3 Copies / Mr Wilkins Devanag. Ms. / Bengalee Ms. / Calcutta Edition." Incidentally, this note also reveals the manuscripts on which the edition was based, and which are not explicitly mentioned in the advertisement to the edition; there it is only said: "To the task of preparing the copy for this impression, little commendation is due. The Calcutta edition already furnished a good text. This, however, has been carefully collated with two manuscript copies. Such additional verses as these supplied have been inserted in their respective places; and where various readings occurred, the most simple has uniformly been preserved."[41] It should also be noted that the loan of Wilkins's manuscript to Hamilton again bears evidence of their close relations.

The *Library Day Book 1801-1814* has preserved a statistical account of the Hitopadeśa edition.[42] From that account we learn that about 500 copies of the "Hitopadesa, Sanskrita. Library Ed." were printed at the Press in the Honorable Company's Library during the years 1809 and 1810. Although the advertisement to the edition is dated December 20, 1810, the first mention of copies leaving the library goes back to December 17, when 25 copies were sent to Haileybury. The College again required 23 copies on February 4, 1811, and later, 4 on February 18, 1813; 9 on February 22, 1813; 10 on February 19, 1814; 50 on April 1, 1814; 50 on January 7, 1815. Some of the copies were sent to the booksellers Black and Co. for public sale: 4 on a date not stated,[43] 10 on February 24, 1814; 2 on January 5, 1815; 10 on January 7, 1815, and 1 on May 11, 1818. Some individual acquirers are also mentioned: Mr Shakespear of the Croydon Seminar[44] on February 11, 1811; Earl Spencer on February 13, 1811; Archduke John for Sir W. Congreve on February 28, 1817, and again Mr Shakespear on June 20, 1818.

Sylvain Lévi, followed by Raymond Schwab, supposes that it was for his edition of the Hitopadeśa that Hamilton went to the National Library in Paris, in 1802: "il préparait une édition du Hitopadeça, l'Esope indien, que Wilkins avait traduit dès 1787. Il désirait collationner les manuscrits de la Bibliothèque nationale à Paris. L'obligeance et l'érudition de Langlès 'garde-interprète des manuscrits orientaux,' étaient connues de tous les orientalistes; un éditeur du Hitopadeça pouvait, plus encore que tout autre, compter sur

[41] P. VI.

[42] P. 38 of the transactions.

[43] Some time between February 13, 1811 and February 18, 1813.

[44] To be precise: Addiscombe, the military college of the East India Company. Shakespear was Oriental professor there.

son concours, car Langlès avait dès 1790, 'sous les auspices de la Liberté,' traduit en français la version de Wilkins, et il y avait ajouté de son cru un 'Discours préliminaire avec des notes sur la religion, la littérature, les moeurs, etc., des Hindous.'"[45] Although this is not impossible, we do not think it really was the case. Whereas there was a manuscript of the Hitopadeśa in Paris,[46] Hamilton used two manuscripts only for his edition, and these, as we know from the extract of the *Library Day Book* cited above, were two London manuscripts. Moreover, we believe that the edition of the Hitopadeśa arose from the need to have a good Sanskrit text for his students at the East India College. If Lévi's hypothesis had been based upon the testimony of one of Hamilton's contemporaries in Paris, we would pay more attention to it; but, as it is, it seems to be due to a rationalization on the part of Lévi, who wanted to find a specific reason for Hamilton's voyage to Paris.

GRAMMATICAL ANALYSIS OF THE HITOPADEŚA

Hamilton also composed a grammatical analysis of the beginning of the Hitopadeśa, going up to page 11, line 13, of his edition. This analysis was not meant to be a book, but a series of notes for the use of his students at Haileybury, and was never made accessible to the public. There is neither title, nor place or date of publication; the volume consisted of 72 pages in-4°, the first of which begins with: "Analysis. Page 1." From the account preserved in the *Library Day Book 1801-1814*,[47] we learn that it was officially called *Grammatical Analysis of the Sanskrita Hitopadesa*, and that about 250 copies were printed in 1810-1811 at the Library Press by Henington. We can even follow the progress of the printing: on November 14, 1810, 20 copies of the first sheet were sent to Haileybury, which were returned; on February 13, 1811, 12 copies of the first 5 sheets were sent to Haileybury, and on August 22, the same number of copies of "4 Sheets succeeding completing the Analysis as far as printed by Henington"; on January 29, 1812, 99 copies of the complete analysis were sent to Haileybury College. There is no mention of a public sale for the *Analysis*; two individuals only are mentioned as having acquired a copy: Mr Ekenstoun on January 29, 1814, and Mr Gordon on October 23, 1818.

CRITICISMS OF THE EDITION AND THE ANALYSIS OF THE HITOPADEŚA

Both the edition and the grammatical analysis of the Hitopadeśa have been the object of criticism by various scholars. There is no doubt that both volumes

[45] *Op. cit.*, p. 338. Cf. also SCHWAB: *op. cit.*, p. 74.

[46] HAMILTON-LANGLES: *op. cit.*, number 141 of the mss. in bengali characters.

[47] P. 38 of the transactions, just after the account for the edition of the Hitopadeśa.

do indeed show real imperfections, but, in our opinion, they sometimes have been pointed out with too much severity.

Langlès writes in 1813: "Il est digne de remarque que l'Hitôpadêsha, l'un des plus anciens ouvrages sanksrits, soit aussi le premier de cette langue imprimé avec des caractères originaux (Dêva-nâgari) dans l'Inde, en 1804, et en Europe, Londres, 1810, 119 pag., in-4°. Cette réimpression a été conférée sur deux manuscrits; elle présente quelques augmentations et quelques variantes, et, en même temps, des fautes assez graves qui sont, pour la plupart, rectifiées dans un long *errata.* On pourrait même regarder comme une erreur typographique le millésime du titre, qui porte en chiffres indiens, 1866, si l'on ne présumait que l'éditeur, qui, sans se nommer, se désigne comme professeur de samskrit au collége de Hailey-Bury, a daté du *Sambat,* c'est-à-dire, de l'ère de Vikramaditya Ier, qui commença l'an 56 avant l'ère chrétienne." [48]

In a letter to Wilhelm von Humboldt, written from London on March 5, 1820, Franz Bopp mentions the two works of Hamilton as the only ones capable of helping the beginner to learn Sanskrit: "Ich habe gar keine Zeit versäumt die Aufträge zu erfüllen, womit mich Ew. Excellenz beehrt haben. Wilkins lässt sich Ew. Excellenz ehrerbietigst empfehlen, bey Uebersendung seiner *Radicals,* die ich bereits Hr. v. Bülow übergeben habe. Auch habe ich Hr. Wilkins bemerkt, dass Hamiltons Analyse des Anfangs des Hitopadêsa Ew. Excellenz vielleicht nützlich seyn könnte, und er übergab mir ebenfalls ein Exemplar, bloss 9 Bogen enthaltend, welches ich zu Hr. von Bülow gebracht. Diese Analyse ist nicht im Verkauf, sondern bloss für das Orientalische Coll. in Hertford verlegt. Indem Ew. Excellenz von Hamiltons Analyse ohne die gedruckte Ausgabe des Hitopadêsa keinen Gebrauch machen könnten, so habe ich Hr. v. Bülow gebeten dieselbe beizufügen, überzeugt, dass ich hierdurch den Wünschen Ew. Excellenz nicht entgegen handeln würde. Ausser den erwähnten Schriften kenne ich keine Elementar-Werke, die das Sanskrit-Studium erleichtern könnten." [49]

The same year, H. Bernstein, in a review of Sanskrit studies, expresses the opinion that the *Analysis* is helpful for beginners only: "Einer kleinen Schrift will ich hier noch gedenken, welche, bloss *Analysis* überschrieben und gar keinen Titel führend, aus 72 Seiten 4to besteht und eine *Analyse* der 11 ersten Seiten der Londoner Ausgabe des *Hitôpadêsa* enthält, mit beständiger Rückweisung auf Wilkins Sanskr. Grammatik. Der Verf. derselben ist *Alexander Hamilton,* vormals Professor zu Hertford, welcher sie für die Schüler im Hertford College vor einigen Jahren in London hat drucken lassen. Sie ist nicht in den Buchhandel gekommen, und für den, welcher über die

[48] *Notice de quelques Ouvrages de Littérature Indienne, publiés au Bengale,* in: *Mercure Etranger* 1, 1813, p. 14.

[49] LEFMANN: *op. cit.,* Nachtrag, pp. 7-8. We shall speak below of Bopp's relations with Hamilton.

Anfangsgründe hinaus ist, ohne Werth, auch nicht ganz fehlerfrey. Ich verdanke sie der Güte eines Freundes." [50]

Hamilton himself was aware of the errors contained in the *Analysis,* as is clear from a letter of Bopp to W. v. Humboldt, dated April 1, 1823: "Die Analyse des Hitop. ist von Hamilton, mit dem ich selber davon gesprochen habe. Er sah nicht gern, dass sie verbreitet würde, weil er wüsste, dass sie mehrere Versehen enthalte." [51] This information was passed on to August Wilhelm Schlegel immediately, but, as is frequent in such cases, it was slightly distorted. Whereas Bopp said that Hamilton did not wish to give his *Analysis* to the public, Humboldt writes that he did not wish to be known as its author: "Ew. Hochwohlgebohrnen legen die Analyse der 12 ersten Seiten des Hitopadesa, die ich auch besitze, dem Professor Haughton bei. Bopp sagte mir immer, die sey von Hamilton, er sehe aber nicht gern, dass man es sage, weil er selbst fühle, dass die Arbeit schwach sey." [52]

In 1825, when he decided to publish a new edition of the Hitopadeśa, A. W. Schlegel sought information about the London edition. In a letter, dated February 28, 1825, to his former student Lassen, then living in London, he writes: "Nicht wahr, Wilkins hat an der Londoner Ausgabe der Hitôp [adêsa] gar keinen Antheil gehabt, sondern sie ganz der Besorgung des verstorbenen Alex[ander] Hamilton überlassen? Ziehen Sie doch hierüber genaue Erkundigungen ein." [53]

On June 23, 1825, Lassen writes from Paris to Schlegel: "Das 4te Buch des Hitôpadêṣa werde ich gleich nach dem Râmây[ana] vornehmen; die gedruckte Ausgabe hoffe ich, wird in der Bibliothek seyn; es freut mich ausserordentlich, dass Ewr. Hochwohlgebohren die Absicht haben, dieses Buch, das Hamilton etwas englisch behandelt hat, neu herauszugeben." [54] It hardly needs to be mentioned that, as far as his disregard for all non-German philological work is concerned, in this passage Lassen shows himself to be a faithful student of his former teacher.

Hamilton's errors, which, as was natural, had already been duly noticed, were now attacked with a typically Schlegelian ardor in the edition of the Hitopadeśa published in 1829 by him and Lassen. Hamilton's name, however, is not quoted. Schlegel writes about the edition: "Editor Londinensis, tametsi pro certo traditum accepi, quis fuerit, quandoquidem nomen suum neque titulo libri, neque praefationi Hayleyburii scriptae apposuit, illud tacere magis aequum arbitror quam divulgare. Etenim laudes occultas in lucem protrahere

[50] *Op. cit.,* col. 2322-2323.

[51] LEFMANN: *op. cit.,* Nachtrag, p. 32.

[52] Albert LEITZMANN (ed.): *Briefwechsel zwischen Wilhelm von Humboldt und August Wilhelm Schlegel,* Halle, 1908, p. 136. The letter is dated April 8, 1823.

[53] W. KIRFEL (ed.): *Briefwechsel A. W. von Schlegel Christian Lassen,* Bonn, 1914, p. 115.

[54] *Ibid.,* pp. 136-137.

et licet et iuvat; secus est in vituperandi necessitate."[55] Lassen, in his turn, attacked the *Analysis*: "Qui in SCHLEGELII nota ad dist. 2 prooem. memoratur commentator Hertfordensis, idem est vir, qui editionem Londinensem molitus est. Commentarius iste, in usum scholarum Hayleyburii habendarum conscriptus, continet pp. LXXII analysin grammaticam Hitopadesae usque ad Lib. I, dist. 33. extensam, Sed nunquam, quod sciam, publici iuris factus est. Quod optime factum esse vel uno specimine demonstrare suffecit./ *hitopadeśo 'yaṃ* | Ed. Lond. *-deśāyaṃ* | Portentosam lectionem silentio praetermisissem, nisi commentator Hertford. eius rationem reddere conatus esset; venditat nimirum istud pro vocabulo composito, quale nunquam formari potuit."[56]

In his *Réflexions sur l'étude des langues asiatiques*, Schlegel comes back to that point with no less severity: "L'édition du Hitôpadêsa, donnée par M. Carey, est remplie de fautes. L'éditeur anonyme de celle de Londres en a corrigé quelques-unes, mais il a introduit une foule de nouvelles fautes. C'est vraiment l'étable d'Augias. L'on ne pourra pas mettre cela sur le compte des imprimeurs. J'ai entre les mains une analyse grammaticale des douze premières pages du Hitôpadêsa, imprimée à l'usage des étudians de Hayleybury: l'éditeur s'y efforce vainement d'expliquer les leçons vicieuses, et il décèle par là son ignorance."[57] In the *Lettre à M. Horace Hayman Wilson*, annexed to these *Réflexions*, Hamilton is explicitly mentioned: "Feu M. Alexandre Hamilton, qui fut en effet le premier professeur de langue sanscrite en Angleterre, remplissait la condition d'avoir acquis ses connaissances dans l'Inde. Il en possédait d'assez étendues en fait de bibliographie, comme le prouve son catalogue de la Bibliothèque royale à Paris. Mais son édition du Hitôpadêsa et son analyse des premières pages de ce livre, décèlent sa faiblesse dans la partie élémentaire, que vous dédaignez si fort, et qui est pourtant la base de tout le reste."[58] It should be remembered, however, that these lines are part of a whole scheme in which Schlegel tries to demonstrate the supremacy of German scholarship as compared to the knowledge acquired in India itself, whose main protagonist was H. H. Wilson. We are far here even from the incidental reference to the help given by Hamilton to his brother Friedrich: "Als mein Bruder seit dem J. 1803 in Paris sich auf die Erlernung des Sanskrit wandte, da war es in der That ein herkulisches Unternehmen in dieser unbetretenen Wildniss sich einen Weg zu bahnen, und in seinen Umgebungen, in seiner Europäischen Entlegenheit von den Quellen des heiligen

[55] Augustus Guilelmus a SCHLEGEL-Christianus LASSEN: *Hitopadesas id est Institutio Salutaris*, Bonn, 1829, part I, p. IX.

[56] *Ibid.*, part II, pp. XIV-XV.

[57] A. W. de SCHLEGEL: *Réflexions sur l'étude des langues asiatiques, adressées à Sir James Mackintosh, suivies d'une lettre à M. Horace Hayman Wilson*, Bonn-Paris, 1832, p. 63; cf. also p. 58.

[58] *Ibid.*, p. 137.

Stromes konnte er mit Recht sagen:/ Avia Pieridum peragro loca, nullius ante / Trita solo, iuvat integros accedere fontes / Glücklicher Weise fand er einen früher am Ganges einheimisch gewordenen Wegweiser. Einige unvollkommene handschriftliche und gedruckte Versuche der Missionare ausgenommen, gab es damals fast noch gar keine Hüfsmittel; man musste unmittelbar von den ersten Elementen der Sprache zur Lesung der Original-Handschriften fortgehen, welche, wie sich versteht, dem Ungeübten weit schwerer zu entziffern sind, als gedruckte Bücher." [59] One should not, however, expect August Wilhelm Schlegel to have been more grateful toward Hamilton for the help the latter gave to Friedrich, than he was toward Bopp for the help he himself had received from him.

A later editor of (part of) the Hitopadeśa, and a later professor of Sanskrit at Haileybury, Francis Johnson, reduces the diatribes of Schlegel and Lassen to their just proportions: "It was, no doubt, this consideration which, almost from the establishment of the East-India College, recommended the *Hitopadeśa* as a class-book, and led to the publication of the text in London. Unfortunately, the task was accomplished with insufficient care, and the edition is disfigured with numerous and serious errors. These have been pointed out in the notes of Professor Lassen to the Bonn edition, with more severity than it perhaps altogether deserved, although, it must be confessed, with undeniable justice. It is now, however, unnecessary to dwell upon the subject, as the edition is exhausted, and its faults may be consigned to oblivion." [60]

In fact, the reason why Schlegel and Lassen found Hamilton's errors monstrous was the same as the reason why Hamilton denied to Paulinus a Sancto Bartholomaeo any knowledge of Sanskrit: the progress of Indian studies was a fast one, and the newcomers were soon far better armed than their predecessors, without sufficiently realizing their debt to them.

SANSKRIT GRAMMATICAL TERMINOLOGY

Alongside with the *Hitopadeśa* and the *Analysis* there also is a third work which was composed by Hamilton for his students at Haileybury. It bears the title *Terms of Sanskrit Grammar* and consists of 13 pages in-4°, printed in London by Cox and Baylis, 75, Great Queen-Street. From the account in the *Library Day Book 1801-1814* [61] we learn that the printing of 200 copies was completed by April 1, 1814, [62] and that 186 of them were sent to Haileybury College on July 25. The *Library Day Book 1814-1820* itself mentions,

[59] *Ueber den gegenwärtigen Zustand der Indischen Philologie*, p. 6.

[60] *Hitopadeśa. The Sanskrit Text of the First Book, or Mitra-lábha; with a grammatical analysis, alphabetically arranged. Prepared for the use of the East-India College*, London, 1840, pp. II-III.

[61] P. 69 of the transactions.

[62] Adelung: *Bibliotheca Sanscrita*, p. 47, is not far from the truth when he gives 1815 as the date of publication.

under the date of December 29, 1819, that copies were presented to Mr Bopp and Mr La Roche.[63]

Gildemeister echoes a controversy about the authorship of this work: "Ejus auctorem fuisse A. HAMILTONEM a Schlegelio accepi, Haugtonem, quod minus probabile, alii perhibuerunt."[64] Schlegel's indication referred to by Gildemeister must have had a private character, since in the *Indische Bibliothek* Schlegel mentions the book without stating Hamilton's name: "Die schätzbarste Zugabe bei dem Buche (= Carey's Sanskrit Grammar) ist eine Abhandlung über die Prosodie, oder vielmehr über die Metrik, und im Anhange die Terminologie der einheimischen Grammatiker mit kurzen Erklärungen. Dieses Verzeichnis ist zwar keineswegs vollständig, es kann aus dem in London gedruckten hier und da ergänzt werden, und zu beiden zusammengenommen wäre noch vieles hinzuzufügen vornämlich aber aus der Denkart der Erfinder mehr ins Licht zu stellen."[65] Schlegel, however, undoubtedly was aware of the true situation, since the catalogue of his private library indicates under the number 321: "(Hamilton), analysis (of the first pages of the Hitopadesa, London edition) s. l. a.—(Eiusd.) Terms of Sanskrit Grammar. London. s. a."[66]

We have not been able to find who attributed the work to Haughton. In any case Haughton cannot have been the author, since the volume was printed in 1814, whereas he did not come back to England until 1815, and did not become an assistant professor at the East India College until 1817.

[63] About La Roche, there is the following note: "Mr La Roche is about to process to Benaras as a Missionary in the employ of the Church Mission Society. He is from Switzerland." Bopp was known well enough.

[64] Joannes GILDEMEISTER: *Bibliothecae Sanskritae sive Recensus librorum sanskritorum hucusque typis vel lapide excriptorum critici Specimen*, Bonn-London, 1847, p. 105.

[65] 2, Bonn, 1827, pp. 18-19.

[66] *Katalog der von Aug. Wilh. von Schlegel nachgelassenen Büchersammlung welche Montag den 1ten Dezember 1845 und an den folgenden Tagen Abends, 5 Uhr präcise bei J. M. Heberle in Bonn öffentlich versteigert und dem Letzbietenden gegen gleich baare Zahlung verabfolgt wird.*

CHAPTER VI

ACTIVITIES OUTSIDE THE EAST INDIA COLLEGE

NEW CONTRIBUTIONS TO THE *EDINBURGH REVIEW*

During Hamilton's prolonged stay in Paris, his Edinburgh friends did not forget him. In a letter to Francis Horner, dated August 8, 1803, Jeffrey complains: "There has been a sad breaking up of the society in which we used to live so pleasantly; Hamilton, and Horner, and Allen, and now the Smiths."[1] After they had created the Friday Club in 1803, they even elected him a member, during his absence, in 1804.[2] This proves that they felt he still belonged to Edinburgh and their society, since the club "was entirely of a literary and social character, and was open, without any practical limitation of numbers, to any person generally resident in Edinburgh, who was supposed to combine a taste for learning or science with agreeable manners, and especially with perfect safety."[3] However, his appointment to the East India College on his return from France prevented Hamilton from settling in Edinburgh again. But the ties with the Edinburgh group remained close, and, almost immediately after his arrival in Great Britain, he renewed his contributions to the *Edinburgh Review*.

It should be noticed that, whereas Hamilton resumed his contributions to the *Edinburgh Review*, he does not seem to have contributed new articles to the *Asiatic Annual Register*. However, we can be sure that there had been no break between him and L. D. Campbell, the editor of the *Asiatic Annual Register*; in 1807, while attacking some articles published in the *Edinburgh Review*, Campbell highly praises Hamilton, without however quoting his name:

"This last discussion must have been perused with mingled sentiments of aversion and regret, by every reader of the Edinburgh Review, who is conversant with the peculiar system of manners, and the internal polity of our Indian fellow-subjects, and who, in the first two numbers of that work, had seen oriental publications reviewed by a writer, thoroughly acquainted with those manners and that polity, as well as deeply versed in the languages, literature, and history of Asia. An unfortunate absence from his country, for a long time deprived the public of the lucubrations of this learned and judicious writer; but he has now resumed his labours in the Edinburgh

[1] Cockburn: *Life of Lord Jeffrey*, vol. II, p. 79.

[2] Cockburn: *An Account of the Friday Club*, p. 114; *Life of Lord Jeffrey*, vol. I, p. 149.

[3] Cockburn: *Life of Lord Jeffrey*, vol. I, p. 148.

Review: and no man, I am persuaded, deprecates more strongly than he does, those speculations on the state of India, in which his critical colleague was pleased to indulge. If, indeed, I could have entertained any doubt as to his sentiments on this point, his review of Mr. Colebrook's book on the *Husbandry and Internal Commerce of Bengal* would have removed it. The reader will find that interesting piece of criticism in the 19th number of the Edinburgh Review, which has just been published: and it particularly claims his attentive consideration, both from the sound principles it contains, and from the striking contrast it exhibits, to the chimerical speculations to which I have adverted."[4]

1806-1807

N. C. Smith states[5] that Hamilton resumed his contributions to the *Edinburgh Review* in its 17th number, published in October 1806. Copinger too, attributes to Hamilton the review of the 7th volume of the *Asiatick Researches*, begun in the 17th number, and continued in the 18th number.[6] Moreover, the very text of the said review does not leave any doubt about the authorship. In his introduction the author refers to his earlier review of the preceeding volume of the *Asiatick Researches* which we have analyzed above. He also gives an account of Oriental research in France during the past few years; whereas he regrets that the French lack the necessary fundamental knowledge on which to base their researches, and have to go on such unreliable sources as Paulinus a Sancto Bartholomaeo, he manifestly has been struck by their eagerness and zeal in the field of Oriental studies:

"In our First Number, we gave an account of the papers which compose the sixth volume of these Transactions. Two additional volumes have since reached this country; and we lament the circumstances which have so long prevented us from examining their contents; knowing, as we do, the interest which the ingenious labors of our countrymen excite here, and still more perhaps on the continent of Europe. In this interval, a translation of the two first volumes of the Asiatic Researches has appeared at Paris, enriched with copious annotations by the celebrated orientalist M. Langlès, conservateur des manuscrits orientaux à la Bibliotheque Imperiale. Although the review of mere translations from English publications does not fall within the scope of our undertaking, yet the successful elucidations and erudition of the annotator might perhaps provoke and justify a deviation from our plan. We should, in that case, find much to applaud, and something to deplore. Of

[4] Lawrence Dundas CAMPBELL: *A Reply to the Strictures of the Edinburgh Review, on the Foreign Policy of Marquis Wellesley's Administration in India; comprising an Examination of the late Transactions in the Carnatic*, London, 1807, p. 9, n.

[5] *Op. cit.*, vol. I, p. 157, n. 4.

[6] In: *Ed. Rev.*, vol. 9, no. 17, October 1806, art. 6, pp. 92-101, and no. 18, January 1807, art. 2, pp. 278-304. *WIVP* attributes both to Hamilton.

the notes, indeed, a great part would appear superfluous in this country, where a considerable portion of the information they contain has been long naturalized and disseminated. Two circumstances, perhaps unavoidable, have contributed to add to their bulk, without augmenting their value. First, many European travellers, and a variety of Mohamedan writers, had attempted to delineate the opinions and manners of the natives of India; but ignorant of the language, which could alone furnish a secure guide to their researches, their disquisitions have seldom presented more than an accumulation of errors. Not sufficiently aware of that circumstance, M. Langlès has frequently been led astray by the multiplicity of his information; a fault from which less general learning would in some measure have secured him. Nothing can be more certain than the remark of Sir William Jones, that if we desire to form correct notions relative to the Hindus, we must begin by forgetting all that has been published respecting them, antecedent to the appearance of Mr Wilkins's translation of the Bhágavat Gita. The second cause, to which may be assigned many erroneous facts and opinions adopted in the work of the learned annotator, is his reliance on the authority of the Roman missionary Fra Paolino de San Bartholomeo. This singular person (whose ignorance of the Sanscrit language, of which he pretended to publish a dictionary, admits of the most unequivocal proof) has thought fit to contradict Sir William Jones, Mr Wilkins, Mr Halhed, and M. Anquetil du Perron, on points of the highest importance, and in terms which even a certainty of being right could not excuse, much less justify. In this discrepancy of authorities, is it wonderful that learned men, personally unacquainted with the facts, should sometimes mistake confident assertion for genuine truth, and arrogant presumption for conscious merit; that the modest and unassuming information of a Jones or a Wilkins, should sometimes give place to the misrepresentations of Fra Paolino?

"Notwithstanding the superior advantages which the English orientalists derive from our establishments in the centre of Asia, it may be doubted, whether the zeal and abilities of our neighbours, devoted to the cultivation of eastern learning, will not compensate that disadvantage; and whether we may not in time have more to learn than to communicate. Since the publication of the work above alluded to, M. Langlès has given the world a second edition of his Dictionary of the language spoken by the Mantchew tartars, to which he has prefixed a dissertation, where their history is traced from the earliest times, till the period when their arms subjugated the empire of China. The same writer is now employed in preparing a complete translation of the Arabian geographers; a work to inspire and to gratify the highest degree of public attention, by presenting the most authentic monuments of the state of the world in the middle ages, when those writers flourished. The justly celebrated academician M. de Lacy[7] has published a dissertation on the ancient

[7] Misprint for Sacy.

history of Arabia, which concludes the long and memorable labours of the Academy of Inscriptions and Belles Lettres. Replete with ingenious criticism, and marked by solid and varied erudition, this memoir will be found highly deserving the attention of all whom such disquisitions can interest. His Chrestomathia Arabica, now in the press, excites expectations proportioned to the high reputation of the writer. A translation of Strabo has appeared at Paris, published at the expence of the government, with copious notes by M. Dutheil. To this work, M. Gosselin, who is considered as a successor worthy of the famous D'Anville, has prefixed a dissertation on the itinerary stadium of the antients . . . M. Chezy, a young orientalist of fair promise, who to a classical taste unites a critical acquaintance with the poets of Arabia and Persia, has attempted to naturalize their productions in France, by a translation of the poetical romance of Mejnun and Leila, composed by the celebrated Jami. But this simple story, which has exercised the talents of so many eastern writers, and which must owe all its merits to description, and the beauty of detail, is little calculated to please the Parisian palate. The moonstruck madness of the hapless Mejnun, and the meek resignation of his lovesick mistress, perpetually reproduced in different positions, are altogether incapable of supporting the attention of this lively people. In works of imagination, their exclusive predilection for the admirable writers of their own country, renders them blind to every other merit. With them, to imitate Corneille, Racine, or Jean Baptiste Rousseau, is to imitate the antients. It is probable, indeed, that these fine writers had the antient in view to a certain degree; but the greater part of their successors limit their ambition to imitating them, without concerning themselves about their models. Hence, probably, originates an exclusive taste for indigenous productions, and, since Shakespeare and Schiller, Milton and Klopstock, are fastidiously rejected by them from the number of great poets, the eastern bards, with faults more striking, and beauties more exotic, stand little chance of success. The romance of Jami would probably be more relished in this country, where we can admire the beauties of our own writers, without limiting poetical excellence to compositions modelled on their style, and fashioned to their manner." [8]

One clearly feels here a man who has lived in France for several years, and is better informed about the French situation than about what happened in Britain. Hamilton even announces a more extensive report of French oriental studies in the future:

"Before we resume an examination of the progress made by our countrymen in Eastern learning, we thought, that to such of our readers as these pursuits interest, a rapid sketch of the contemporaneous labours of the French oriental-

[8] In: *Ed. Rev.*, vol. 9, pp. 92-94.

ists might not prove unacceptable. Of these, in all probability, a more correct account will be exhibited in our future pages." [9]

There is, however, nothing more to be read on this subject in the following issues of the *Edinburgh Review.*

Another interesting indication is the fact that, in contradiction to the general rule in the *Edinburgh Review,* the article is written in two parts. The reason obviously is that Hamilton returned to Great Britain too late to write a complete review of the *Asiatick Researches* in the number for October 1806.

Coming to the actual review of the *Asiatic Researches,* Hamilton regrets that the system of orthography (transliteration) of William Jones is not maintained in this volume:

"Prefixed to the seventh volume of the Asiatic Researches, we find a list of 'Desiderata,' proposed to the industry of the learned. The perusal of it excited a melancholy reflection on the short-lived authority of the most celebrated names. We there find the orthography proposed and laboriously discussed by Sir William Jones, in his introductory dissertation, entirely laid aside. Its advantages, indeed, can be appreciated only by persons conversant with the Oriental languages." [10]

As far as he himself is concerned, he will invariably use William Jones's system:

"We beg leave to mention, that, in future reviews of Oriental publications, we will scrupulously adhere to the orthography of Sir William Jones, in writing proper names; and, even in our extracts, take the liberty of adapting them to that model, if ignorance or caprice should have induced our authors to spell them differently." [11]

In his review of the article by Mahony: *On Singhálá, or Ceylon, and the Doctrines of Buddha, from the Books of the Singhálá,* he again reveals himself as somebody who has come from Paris:

"we take leave to subjoin an abridged translation of the third chapter of the Bhágavat, of which two copies are deposited in the Imperial library at Paris." [12]

This article also leads him to a hypothesis, which he is to defend several times later, namely that:

[9] *Ibid.*, p. 94.
[10] *Ibid.*, p. 95.
[11] *Ibid.*, p. 95, n.
[12] *Ibid.*, p. 98.

"notwithstanding their rejection of the Vedá, the Buddhists are genuine Vaïsnava, or adorers of Visnu."[13]

The article by J. T. Blunt: *Narrative of a Route from Chunarghur to Yertnagoodum, in the Ellar sircar* is an occasion for Hamilton to state his arguments against the theory that the tribes of mountaineers would be totally different from the Hindus in origin, language and religion.

To the *Translation of one of the Inscriptions on the Pillar at Delhi, called the Lat of Firuz Khan,* by H. T. Colebrooke; with *Introductory Remarks* by Harington, Hamilton objects that it is too exclusively descriptive. As "such monuments are only useful in illustrating history,"[14] the translators should have payed more attention to the historical data which can be drawn from them. And, in illustrating that point, Hamilton goes to the extent of translating a passage from Abu'l Fazl. Translations of the same author had already appeared and were later to appear in Hamilton's reviews.

The *Account of the Cucis, or Lunctas,* by John Macrae gives him an opportunity to recall the meetings of the Asiatic Society in Calcutta and, at the same time, the meetings of the Institut de France in Paris:

"The anniversary discourses of Sir William Jones supplied an important *desideratum,* by indicating and generalizing the most prominent facts discovered since the last. Such a summary by the eloquent and philosophic Cuvier, usually forms the most interesting portion of the labour of the French Institute."[15]

The article by H. T. Colebrooke: *On the Sanscrit and Prácrit Languages* attracted Hamilton's special attention. Of the various languages treated by Colebrooke, he gave a different classification, not however without explicitly stating his great admiration for Colebrooke's learning:

"Notwithstanding our extreme deference for the superior attainments of Mr Colebrooke in the Sanscrit language, we venture to doubt the accuracy of his conclusion; and to contend for the actual existence, as spoken languages, of all enumerated."[16]

Colebrooke's articles *On the Religious Ceremonies of the Hindus, and of the Brahmans especially* also provoked Hamilton's remarks. It is noteworthy that, although Hamilton shows an evident respect for Colebrooke, he frequently disagrees with him; he is undoubtedly much more attracted by Wilkins's personality than by Colebrooke's:

"To the candour of Mr Colebrooke, in retracting the incidental mistakes he had fallen into in former essays, we cannot assign too much praise. We

[13] *Ibid.,* p. 98.
[14] *Ibid.,* p. 284.
[15] *Ibid.,* p. 287.
[16] *Ibid.,* p. 289.

must, however, enter our protest against another practice, into which he appears to have been inadvertently led, and which, in the present state of imperfect information on the subject of Indian history, may be productive of infinite confusion and perplexity. It is the incidental mention, in notes, of important and sometimes singular opinions, unsupported by evidence, and leading to no discussion. Erroneous ideas once disseminated are not easily extirpated; and the interests of truth and science are better consulted by weighing probabilities, where positive evidence cannot be procured, than in circulating unexamined possibilities." [17]

The article *On the Religion and Manners of the People of Ceylon,* by Joinville, furnishes a new occasion to contest the claim that Buddhism is prior to Brahmanism, and to warn scholars against writing about Oriental antiquities without a sufficient knowledge of the language:

"We would earnestly recommend to such of our countrymen as have leisure for such researches, to attend first to the natural history, the population, the commerce, the civil and military institutions of the country; in short, every thing comprised in its actual situation. But, if these barriers be too confined for the activity of their exertions, and researches into antiquities furnish a more alluring field, we shall then intreat them to begin with the study of the Páli, or at least of the Singhaleze language. The miserable errors of all the disquisitions composed by learned Europeans on the subject of Hindu antiquities, before the Sanscrit language was studied, holds out a salutary admonition to our countrymen in Ceylon, and should prevent them from publishing what, a few years later, will be recognized as errors, or neglected as futile." [18]

His review of *An Account of the Bazigars, a Sect commonly denominated Nuts* by David Richardson shows a deep insight on his part in the language of the Gipsies:

"Captain Richardson describes the manners of several tribes of itinerant jugglers, who gain a livelihood by exhibiting their tribes and gambols for pay, throughout Hindustan. In their love of intoxication, dissolute habits, and indifference for all religion, they resemble the Gipsies; and the language of the latter is most unquestionably derived from India. We have examined, with attention, the vocabulary of the Gipsies, published by Grellman; and half of the words are obviously of Indian origin; many Persian words also occur, and several German and Italian. We are inclined to think that the remainder will be found to be Turkish and Slavonic, all amassed in the course of their migrations. They gave out in Italy that they were Egyptians flying from the persecution of the Saracens; but this story was much questioned at

[17] *Ibid.,* p. 295.

[18] *Ibid.,* pp. 301-302.

the time, as invented to excite compassion. Those who arrived in Hungary and Bohemia do not appear to have made that presentation, and came there from the provinces adjacent to the Black Sea. It were curious to ascertain the period of their quitting India. It struck us, that the word *banduc,* a musket, established their emigration to be posterior to the invention of fire arms. But we are informed that this term is in use through the whole Turkish dominion. Many Sanscrit words occur in their vocabulary, which have never been adopted into Hindustani; and the Persian words might be owing to their transit through that country, as the German and the Italian undoubtedly are. *Náta,* of which *Nut* is a corruption, signifies a dancer, in Sanscrit." [19]

Copinger also attributes to Hamilton the review of *Les Templiers, Tragédie, précédée d'un Précis Historique sur les Templiers* by F. J. M. Raynouard, in the 17th number of the *Edinburgh Review.*[20] We do not think that this attribution can be correct. Indeed, some passages exclude the possibility of the author's having been in Paris recently:

"When we first were informed that the tragedy of the Templars had been represented with considerable success at Paris, we became anxious to obtain a copy of it. Within a few days of the time when we are now writing, this publication was put into our hands. The task of reviewing it has been greater than we reckoned so far, as we did not expect to get a history into the bargain," [21]

and also:

"The allusion in the last lines was probably applauded at Paris." [22]

The review also contains a description of the English public's attitude in the theaters; this can hardly be expected from somebody who had been absent from England for several years.

The 10th volume of the *Edinburgh Review* contains a review of Colebrooke's treatise: *Remarks on the Husbandry and Internal Commerce of Bengal,*[23] which must be attributed to Hamilton. L. D. Campbell had no doubt about the authorship of this article, as we have seen above. Moreover, in a review of Wilks's *Historical Sketches of the South of India* [24]—certainly by Hamilton, as we shall see later—the author engages in a refutation of Wilks's criticisms

[19] *Ibid.,* pp. 303-304.

[20] Vol. 9, no. 17, art. 14, pp. 196-211. *WIVP* does not know of any other testimony confirming this attribution.

[21] *Ibid.,* p. 205.

[22] *Ibid.,* pp. 210-211.

[23] No. 19, April 1807, art. 2, pp. 27-40. Attributed to Hamilton by *WIVP.*

[24] In: *Ed. Rev.,* vol. 18, August 1811, pp. 357-358.

against some earlier statements of his, that were made in the review of Colebrooke's *Remarks.* And, in the review of the 10th volume of the *Asiatick Researches,*[25] which, as we shall see, must also be attributed to Hamilton, the author again makes a reference to his earlier review of Colebrooke's treatise.

The attribution to Hamilton of the review of Colebrooke's book could, at first sight, be contested in view of the following sentence: "We have already remarked that this work was not unknown to Dr Tennant, for whom plagiarism has sometimes furnished an Indian recreation."[26] This passage refers to a review of Tennant's *Indian Recreations,* which appeared in the 4th volume of the *Edinburg Review,* in July 1804,[27] *i. e.* during Hamilton's absence from Great Britain. Hence, the review of Tennant's book cannot possibly have been written by Hamilton—Copinger attributes it to J. Soch (in fact: James Loch)—. If the author of the two reviews were the same, it therefore could not be Hamilton. A study of the two reviews, however, proves that they were written by two different persons: whereas the reviewer of Tennant's work condemns the Hindu methods of husbandry, the reviewer of Colebrooke's vindicates Hindu agriculture against Colebrooke's charges. We consequently may conclude that, if Hamilton could not have been the reviewer of Tennant's work, he could very well have been the reviewer of Colebrooke's treatise. How then, shall we account for the reference quoted above to the review of Tennant's *Indian Recreations*? We venture the hypothesis that here—as it often happens to the articles in the *Edinburgh Review*—Hamilton's review, when passed on to the editor—possibly Jeffrey—was extended with a few introductory remarks of a general nature. We are inclined to believe that the transition from one author to the other is at about the middle of p. 29. The change in tone there is apparent: after very general considerations, we come, rather abruptly, to the point, *i. e.* a matter of fact study of Bengali agriculture.

The reviewer of Tennant's *Indian Recreations* gave the following picture of Hindu agriculture:

"The agriculture of the Hindûs is wretched in the extreme. The rudeness of their implements, the slovenliness of their practice, and their total ignorance of the most simple principles of the science, are all equally remarkable. The husbandry of the South of Europe is bad; but, when compared to that of India, it is perfection. Amidst the ignorance and poverty which disgrace the once fertile provinces of Spain and Italy, we find traces of their former excellence, and we can, without difficulty, perceive in their tools the resemblance of those which were in use two thousand years ago. No such traces of former superiority are displayed in the husbandry of India; and the

[25] In: *Ed. Rev.,* vol. 16, August 1810, p. 387.

[26] In: *Ed. Rev.,* vol. 10, p. 27.

[27] *Ibid.,* pp. 303-329.

rudeness and unfitness of all their implements is a most curious instance of want of contrivance and ingenuity, in a people who have arrived at a certain degree of civilization." [28]

This description was based upon the data given by Tennant in the book under review. In fact, Tennant had drawn much material from the then unpublished treatise of Colebrooke. Colebrooke is not favorable at all to Indian agriculture, but Hamilton tries on the contrary

"to prove that the Bengal peasantry do not proceed without fixed principles for their guidance, and those probably derived from a remote antiquity, and possibly the best adapted to their soil and climate." [29]

Here too, Hamilton shows that he has just returned from France. Speaking of the fact that the British were not allowed to own land in India, he says:

"It is difficult to describe the astonishment with which foreigners learn this act of magnanimity in the British Legislature. Several persons of distinction in France could not conceal the impression produced by mentioning it." [30]

Copinger attributes to Hamilton another contribution to the 10th volume of the *Edinburgh Review*: the review of the article written by J. Bentley in the 8th volume of the *Asiatick Researches: On the Hindoo Systems of Astronomy, and their Connexion with History in Ancient and Modern Times.*[31] We cannot accept this attribution. Indeed, the review of Bentley's article is written from a purely astronomical point of view. A former article of Bentley's in the 6th volume of the *Asiatick Researches* had been criticized by Hamilton in the 1st volume of the *Edinburgh Review*, as we have seen above. Bentley's new article replies to these criticisms. This provokes another reply in the *Edinburgh Review*, but this time by an astronomer—probably Playfair—:

"The paper before us is directed to the same object, and contains also some strictures on an article in our review, where some of the arguments contained in the former paper were shown, as we imagined, to be inconclusive.

"Our intention, at present, is to consider the antiquity of the Indian tables, purely as an astronomical question, and without reference to any other matter in the history or mythology of Hindostan"; [32]

[28] In: *Ed. Rev.*, vol. 4, July 1804, p. 319.

[29] In: *Ed. Rev.*, vol. 10, p. 37.

[30] *Ibid.*, p. 40, n.

[31] In: *Ed. Rev.*, vol. 10, no. 20, July 1807, art. 12, pp. 455-471. Attributed to Playfair by *WIVP*. *WIVP* attributes to Hamilton the review of Waring's *Tour to Shiraz* in *Ed. Rev.*, vol. 10, no. 19, April 1807, art. 4, pp. 61-72, where internal evidence does not allow to draw any conclusion.

[32] *Ibid.*, pp. 456-457.

again:

"we shall now take the liberty of examining Mr Bentley's papers, on principles purely astronomical,"[33]

and finally:

"With respect to the evidence derived from other sources, from the written or the traditionary history of Hindostan, we abstain from any opinion at present, and leave it as a discussion more properly belonging to the antiquary than the astronomer."[34]

1808

The discussion "belonging to the antiquary" announced by the astronomer forms part of the review of the whole volume of the *Asiatick Researches* in the 12th volume of the *Edinburgh Review*.[35]

The authorship of this review constitutes no problem. The very text of the article reveals Hamilton to be the author. Moreover, there are references to preceding reviews which undoubtedly are by his hand: the reviews of the 6th volume of the *Asiatick Researches* and of Anquetil's *Oupnekhat* in the 1st volume of the *Edinburgh Review*, and of the 7th volume of the *Asiatick Researches* in the 9th volume of the *Edinburgh Review*. Moreover, the author quotes the Bhāgavata Purāṇa according to "a copy of that work in the Imperial Library at Paris."[36]

Hamilton's review of Bentley's article again expresses the same objections which had already been raised in the review of Bentley's article contained in the 6th volume of the *Asiatick Researches*. In this review, Bentley's thesis is not examined from an astronomical point of view. The main points under discussion are the antiquity of the Purāṇas and the problem of the interpolations they contain.

In his review of the article by J. D. Patterson: *On the Origin of the Hindu Religion* Hamilton shows himself to be well in agreement with William Jones's line of thought and with the comparativism of his time:

"Iswara and Baghesa are two names for an Indian divinity, whose emblem is the phallus, whose rites consist in its worship: wrapped in a tiger's skin, and mounted on a sacred bull, the personification of Justice, he is followed by a mixed crowd of male and female votaries, whose wild dances and frantic revels accompany his steps, or announce his presence. The meaning of this symbol may be uncertain, and furnish abundant room for ingenious discussion;

[33] *Ibid.*, p. 457.
[34] *Ibid.*, p. 463.
[35] No. 23, April 1808, art. 2, pp. 36-50. Attributed to Hamilton by *WIVP*.
[36] *Ibid.*, p. 48.

but no candid enquirer can doubt, that the Egyptians and Greeks worshipped the same divinity under the appellations of Osiris and of Bacchus. The complete identity of emblems and rites excludes all scepticism on this point. Now, it will not be contended, that the facts or allegories celebrated by those apparently arbitrary attributes, rites and emblems, have a natural application so manifest, that distant nations might each have invented the same ritual. It follows, that they have been borrowed; and the fact of an antient connexion between India and Egypt results as an incontestable deduction from the investigation."[37]

The article *An Essay on the Sacred Isles in the West, with other Essays connected with that Work* affords him a new opportunity to dissent with its author, Wilford. He cannot accept Wilford's thesis according to which the white islands of the Purāṇas would be Great Britain and Ireland:

"The treatise which is to contain the proofs of so remarkable a fact, is postponed to another volume. We by no means wish to prejudge it: like all this gentleman's productions, it will certainly prove learned and ingenious; and however much it may fail in establishing so wonderful a proposition, we are convinced it will abound in collateral information, in classical allusions, and in verbal analogies. We have only to hope, that the latter do not enter for a considerable share in the proofs, that Albion is the white island of the Pauranica geographers."[38]

Once again, the ancient Hindu geography as contained in the Purāṇas apparently is a topic he particularly enjoys:

"Each Purána contains a book on the subject, entitled Bhuvana Cosa, or, Dictionary of Countries. The plan we should have been disposed to recommend would be, to select the most detailed of these compositions; for instance, that in the Váyu, and, after having furnished a literal translation, to add, in the form of annotations, the modern names of all the places mentioned, as far as these can be ascertained, with the authorities for each."[39]

He proceeds to give an example of such a research:

"we venture to exhibit the outlines of the geography of Jambu dwipa, as collected from several concurrent Puránas."[40]

After having given this description, Hamilton contemplated presenting another chapter of ancient geography in a subsequent article:

[37] *Ibid.*, pp. 38-39.
[38] *Ibid.*, p. 36.
[39] *Ibid.*, p. 44.
[40] *Ibid.*, p. 44.

"If our view of the Jambu be correct, it will materially contribute to fix our ideas concerning the others, when we shall find occasion to resume the discussion." [41]

H. T. Colebrooke's article: *On the Vedás, or Sacred Writings of the Hindus* excites his enthusiasm:

"The treatise of which we have now to speak, is, from its subject, the most curious, and from the ability, candour, and research displayed by its author, the most entitled to approbation, of any that have hitherto appeared in the Asiatic Researches. The Vedás, of which some doubted the existence, many the authenticity, and still more the intelligibility, have been in great part collected and perused by Mr Colebrooke, who supports their authenticity by arguments which to us appear irrefragable." [42]

And he immediately thinks of the reaction which this article will awaken in France:

"The literati of the Continent, who have long considered the neglect of this inquiry as a subject for national reproach, will do justice to the luminous though concise view of their contents here exhibited; and the ideas of all will be fixed in respect to their importance to literature." [43]

The 13th volume of the *Edinburgh Review* contains a review of Francis Buchanan's book: *A Journey from Madras, through the Countries of Mysore, Canara and Malabar*,[44] which, with Copinger, we attribute to Hamilton. Indeed, we find back in these pages some of Hamilton's favorite themes, such as the flourishing state which the Hindu cities enjoyed before the Mohammedan invasions, and the idea that Buddhists are Vaiṣṇavas, except for their rejection of the Vedas. Moreover, the author of this review acknowledges that he published in the *Asiatic Annual Register* a translation from Persian of a description of Vijayanagar, which will again be mentioned in the review of Wilks's *Historical Sketches of the South of India*, and which we analyzed above.

Hamilton's opinion of Buchanan is the same as the one he expressed earlier in his review of an article Buchanan published in the 6th volume of the *Asiatick Researches*, a review which we have considered above. Hamilton insists that, in spite of all his abilities and efforts, Buchanan could not obtain, as far as Indian culture is concerned, the data he tried to arrive at. He mentions errors which derive "from his want of acquaintance with the lan-

[41] *Ibid.*, pp. 46-47.
[42] *Ibid.*, p. 47.
[43] *Ibid.*, p. 47.
[44] No. 25, October 1808, art. 6, pp. 82-100. Attributed to Hamilton by *WIVP*.

guages."[45] Moreover, Buchanan's mission made him move his camp all the time, and he never could settle anywhere long enough to become acquainted with the situation he reports. Hamilton, therefore, once again and for the same reasons censures the unfavorable account which Buchanan gave of Brahmanical culture:

"Whenever, therefore, a very worthy man has adopted unfavourable impressions of a whole people, we should first enquire into his opportunities of knowing them. We have no hesitation in stating the faculty of conversing with them as an indispensable qualification; and of this Dr Buchanan was totally destitute.

"When we read the valuable productions of those great Oriental scholars, whose attainments have placed England on a footing with the Continent in that particular,—those of a Jones, a Wilkins, a Colebrooke, or a Halhed,—we uniformly discover in the Hindus a nation, whose polished manners are the result of a mild disposition and an extensive benevolence. But did the long and habitual intercourse with the natives of India, which enabled those eminent writers to acquire such attainments, qualify or disqualify them from forming correct opinions on national character? Is ignorance of individuals the surest method of judging rightly of the mass? We will venture to do justice to those exquisitely cunning priests the Brahmans. It should be recollected, that this appellation is that of a cast, and not of a profession. Three fourths of the sons of Brahma are engaged in secular business, and in no shape distinguished from other laymen, but by a somewhat better education. The remainder are employed as family priests, and in the cultivation of Indian literature. These men are never seen by Europeans, unless sent for; they know nothing of what is passing in the world; their studies include antient history, metaphysics and logic; and letters may be considered there in the same state as in Europe during the middle ages, excepting that the laity possess all the accomplishments necessary for conducting civil occupations, and only have recourse to their priests in matters connected with religious rites. From this retirement, and disengagement from secular concerns, one would naturally infer, that these Brahmans must be singularly disqualified from conducting intrigues. In point of fact, we venture to appeal to all whose personal acquaintance with these calumniated men enables them to decide on the question, whether they have not uniformly found this class of Brahmans, the most candid, the most artless, and the most simple of mankind. We believe that, in all countries, it may be correct to assert, that the individuals who obtrude themselves on the notice of the great, and of strangers,—who beset their steps, watch their motions, and are constantly in view, are the most worthless part of every community. Conscious merit

[45] *Ibid.*, p. 93.

waits to be sought; disinterestedness and probity show no *empressemens.* They seldom obtrude themselves on the attention, and, by superficial observers, always remain undiscovered."[46]

1809

For the review of Wilkins's book: *A Grammar of the Sanskrita Language,* in the 13th volume of the *Edinburgh Review,*[47] we have overwhelming evidence that it was written by Hamilton. Copinger and the article of Chambers-Norman quoted in the introduction hint no doubt about the authorship. Moreover, in a letter written to his daughter Lady Holland on March 7, 1809, Sydney Smith says: "I hope you like the last number of the Edinburgh Review; it is the best I think which has appeared for a long time," and, among the articles he enumerates, figures "Sanskrit Grammar by Hamilton."[48] In the text of the review itself, Hamilton refers to his former review of the 7th volume of the *Asiatick Researches,* and exhibits a thorough acquaintance with the recent developments of Indian studies in France, even of projects which did not lead to any publication, as in the following passage, where he most probably points to Langlès:

"The profuse encouragement given by the present ruler of France to all works calculated to diffuse a knowledge of the oriental languages in his dominions, induced a celebrated French orientalist to examine, in 1805, the manuscript grammars transmitted by the Indian missionaries to the Royal library. But the materials were not found sufficiently ample to recommend the publication to the patronage of government."[49]

The place which Wilkins's grammar occupies in this article is reduced to a few considerations about the knowledge which the West has acquired of Sanskrit, and the value of Wilkins's grammar in this context. The main object of this article is to prove the utility of the knowledge of Sanskrit. According to Hamilton, a knowledge of the Sanskrit language facilitates the learning of modern vernaculars, which derive from it—a point on which he insists in several of his writings—; it is also interesting from a literary point of view, and, in this respect, he refers to William Jones's works; moreover it is important not only as far as India itself is concerned, but also for all the nations east of the Indus; and, finally, comes the point which will be specially developed in the article: Sanskrit is important because of its analogy with other languages. His thesis has been directly inspired by William Jones:

[46] *Ibid.,* pp. 91-92.
[47] No. 26, January 1809, art. 6, pp. 366-381. Attributed to Hamilton by *WIVP.*
[48] N. C. SMITH: *The Letters of Sydney Smith,* vol. I, p. 157.
[49] In: *Ed. Rev.,* vol. 13, p. 366.

"The proposition which the writer of this article would have wished to illustrate, is thus stated by that great philologer, whose critical knowledge of most of the languages mentioned, entitled his opinion to a degree of authority, which the present disquisition is far from claiming. 'That the first race of Persians and Indians,' says Sir William Jones, 'to whom we may add the *Romans* and *Greeks*, the *Goths* and the old *Egyptians* or Ethiops, originally spoke the same language, and professed the same popular faith, is capable, in my humble opinion, of incontestable proof: that the *Jews* and *Arabs*, the *Assyrians* or second Persian race, the people who spoke Syriac, and a numerous tribe of *Abyssinians*, used one primitive dialect, wholly distinct from the idiom just mentioned, is, I believe, undisputed, and, I am sure, indisputable.'"[50]

It is interesting, however, to remark that the erroneous classification which William Jones adopts with regard to Egyptian is not accepted by Hamilton. In his review of the 8th volume of the *Asiatick Researches*, indeed, he had distinctly said:

"The great analogy between the antient languages of India and of Greece has been often and justly remarked; the scanty remains of the antient Egyptian indicate no such affinity, and seem, indeed, more referable to the Hebraic or Arabian source."[51]

In view of the demonstration he undertakes, Hamilton modestly refers to his qualifications:

"To demonstrate this proposition in its whole extent, would have required all the erudition of that celebrated writer; and he who now ventures partially to supply the demonstration, is acquainted, and that very imperfectly, with only a few of the languages which the proposition embraces. To the science of philology he has never devoted a moment; of Greek, his knowledge is slender; and of Hebrew and Ethiopic he is equally and totally ignorant. His sole qualifications for the task he has undertaken, are a tolerable knowledge of Sanscrit, Arabic, Latin, German, and the modern language of Persia. It would have been easy, by the help of lexicons, to have palliated, and perhaps to have concealed this deficiency; but, unambitious of the reputation of a linguist, though desirous of demonstrating a proposition no less true than wonderful, he prefers candidly stating the extent of his qualifications."[52]

We do not intend to study here the detail of Hamilton's linguistic comparisons. This has been the aim of the excellent article by Chambers and

[50] *Ibid.*, p. 371.
[51] In: *Ed. Rev.*, vol. 12, April 1808, p. 39.
[52] In: *Ed. Rev.*, vol. 13, p. 371.

Norman quoted above; these scholars, through a minute comparison with Friedrich Schlegel's book *Ueber die Sprache und Weisheit der Indier,* which Hamilton could not have read at the moment of his review, have shown that a great many of the examples given in both works are the same, and that, in such circumstances, the question of influence must be solved in Hamilton's favor rather than in Schlegel's. The pages we devoted to the relationship between Schlegel and Hamilton in Paris undoubtedly give new support to this thesis.

Rather than go into details, we shall restrict ourselves to quoting a few passages which illustrate the high quality of Hamilton's method. First of all, we want to stress the fact that Hamilton is not satisfied with a simple analogy of words; he already thinks in terms of structure (*i. e.* essentially morphology):

> "The analogy we propose to demonstrate is, in the first place, that of the *words* composing the languages treated of; and secondly, that of their *structure*."[53]

As far as the verbal analogies are concerned, Hamilton already clearly distinguishes between etymologically related words and mere borrowings:

> "In the execution of the first part, we shall merely open the Persic dictionary Farhang Jehanghiri; and, when we meet with a word that has the same signification in Sanscrit, Latin or German, write them in a line. Others will certainly occur in the course of the operation. The number of words to be exhibited will amply demonstrate the analogy; but it is not their number, merely, to which we would direct the attention of our readers. That is unavoidably limited by the nature of our review; and, with a very inconsiderable portion of time and labour, might easily be extended to ten times its present amount. It is the sort, and not the number of similar words that attest the affiliation of consanguinity of nations and languages. In the diffusion of arts and sciences—in the progress of conquests—in the intercourse of commerce, words are imported into every country, which prove no original affinity between the nation which adopts, and that which invented them. Thus, the Greeks have bequeathed to the rest of Europe their sciences and the names of them. Our word 'geography' only proves that science to have been cultivated previously in Greece; 'algebra,' that the Arabs invented the science, and the word to express it; 'alcove,' that this formed a part of Moorish architecture; 'guitare, cithara, or xitarra,' that the instrument was of Persian invention, and originally consisted of *three* strings. To the American Indians, we are indebted for the most useless and the most useful of plants, together with their names, 'tobacco and potatoes.' In the history of arts, sciences, or com-

[53] *Ibid.*, p. 372.

merce, attention to these names may have its utility: in the history of nations, they authorize no deduction whatever.

"On the other hand, there are things which must have been named in the very infancy of society, and before the first dawn of civilization. Where these names correspond, therefore, in different countries, we may confidently infer, that the one has been peopled from the same stock with the other. Thus, the names of the parts of the human body, of the relations of consanguinity, and of the animals most familiar to man, constitute a class of words, without which we cannot suppose mankind to exist even in the rudest state of society. To adopt the hypothesis of the learned Bayer, we must suppose the inhabitants of Hindustan to have waited till Alexander the Great conquered Bactria, in order to obtain appellations for the most endearing ties of nature, and to enable them to express the venerable relations of father and mother. The words we propose to exhibit, consist solely of the class we have described; and it would be superfluous to insert the Arabic words, since our general remark applies to the whole—that the signification of each word cited, is expressed, in Arabic, by sounds totally *dissimilar*." [54]

Copinger also attributes to Hamilton the review of the anonymous work: *An Examination of the Causes which led to the late Expedition against Copenhagen,* in the 13th volume of the *Edinburgh Review*.[55] In the text of the article itself, nothing points to Hamilton: it is purely political.

Volume 14 of the *Edinburgh Review* contains a review of Charles Stewart's *Descriptive Catalogue of the Oriental Library of the late Tippoo Sultan of Mysore,*[56] which must be attributed to Hamilton. The author of the review refers to a translation from Persian (analyzed above) of an episode of Haidar's life to which he later refers in a review of Wilks's *Historical Sketches of the South of India.* Moreover, it is but natural that Hamilton should wish to review a work published by his colleague in the Oriental Department at the East India College.

This review contains nothing particularly interesting. Perhaps it should be noted that the theme of the civilizing role of the Hindus towards their Mohammedan conquerers is once again discussed:

"The mild and benevolent spirit of the Hindu institutions and manners, seems to have softened in Hindustan the turbulent intolerance of Islamism." [57]

The 15th volume of the *Edinburgh Review* includes a new review of the *Asiatick Researches,* this time of the 9th volume.[58] There can be no doubt

[54] *Ibid.*, pp. 372-373.

[55] No. 26, January 1809, art. 13, pp. 488-499. Attributed to Brougham by *WIVP*.

[56] No. 28, July 1809, art. 3, pp. 322-332. No attribution in *WIVP*.

[57] *Ibid.*, p. 327.

[58] No. 29, October 1809, art. 12, pp. 175-189. Attributed to Hamilton by *WIVP*.

about Hamilton's authorship. There are references to his earlier review of the 8th volume of the *Asiatick Researches*, and some of his favorite themes appear here again.

Two articles only in this volume of the *Asiatick Researches* are dealt with in some detail: the continuation of Wilford's *Essay on the Sacred Isles in the West, with other Essays connected with that Work*, and *An Account of the Jains*, which is jointly a work by Mackenzie, Buchanan and Colebrooke. To the first of these articles Hamilton's objections remain the same as in the past. On the occasion of the second article, he once again discusses the relationship and the comparative date of the different sects that existed in India, which he sums up in the following terms:

"To conclude, we think it probable that the worship of Baghes, Iswara or Siva, (the Bacchus and Osiris of the western world), was the first which prevailed in India; that the worship of Visnu or Jupiter, in his supposed incarnation Hericrisna, (or Hercules), was introduced when Vyasa compiled or composed the Vedas; and that the doctrines of Buddha were not promulgated till a considerable time subsequent to the latter period."[59]

He concludes his article by congratulating the editors for the uniform orthography observed, and announces a review of the 10th volume of the *Asiatick Researches* in the next number of the *Edinburgh Review*.

1810

The announced review of the 10th volume of the *Asiatick Researches* did not appear in the following number but in the next volume of the *Edinburgh Review*.[60] The authorship of this review cannot be in doubt. Hamilton makes several references to earlier articles of his, which we shall however not enumerate in detail here; it will be enough to quote a more general reference to his earlier reviews of the successive volumes of the *Asiatick Researches*:

"Those who have followed us through our remarks on the Asiatic Researches, are already sufficiently acquainted with the peculiarities of Captain Wilford's manner,"[61]

and also:

"In reviewing the successive volumes of this interesting publication, we endeavour steadfastly to adhere to our original plan of marking the progressive extension of the boundaries of science, by the labours of this learned society."[62]

[59] *Ibid.*, pp. 186-187.
[60] Vol. 16, no. 32, August 1810, art. 6, pp. 384-398. Attributed to Hamilton by *WIVP*.
[61] *Ibid.*, p. 387.
[62] *Ibid.*, p. 398.

Three articles only are reviewed in detail. About W. Carey's *Remarks on the State of Agriculture in the District of Dinājpur* Hamilton keeps in line with what he said in his review of Colebrooke's treatise already mentioned. He is confident about the effect of Cornwallis's measures:

"It is certainly an interesting speculation to inquire, whether government should take any, and what steps, to remedy the evils complained of, in addition to the salutary effects which may naturally be expected to result from the permanent settlement of the revenue accomplished by Lord Cornwallis." [63]

The continuation of Wilford's *Essay on the Sacred Isles in the West and other Essays connected with that Work* is treated with Hamilton's usual criticism.

The article by J. Leyden: *On the Language and Literature of the Indo-Chinese Nations* gives a new opportunity for Hamilton to show his sound methods of comparative philology, even if the filiation he advances for Persian has now proved wrong:

"Dr Leyden has published a variety of specimens of most of these languages, in order to exhibit the affinity or discrepancy which subsists between them. From the meager vocabulary of two barbarous nations, to whom taste and cultivation have never imparted copiousness of terms, choice of epithets, or variety of expression, words indiscriminately selected may possibly answer the purpose intended. But, such is the copiousness of the language of a literary and civilized people, that indiscriminate selection can lead to no rational conclusion. Or, perhaps, we shall express ourselves more correctly, in saying, that such a comparison may serve to prove an analogy, but cannot prove the contrary, unless the words cited are destitute of synonyms; a fact, in such cases, difficult to ascertain. The modern Persic is indisputably a derivative of Sanscrit, through the medium of the antient Zend. This might easily be proved, by selecting a long vocabulary of words in both languages, similar in sound and meaning. But, as all Persian words are not derived from the same source, it would prove equally easy to produce a list as long, of words of the same signification, but destitute of analogy in sound. Thus, too, our own language might be derived either from the Gothic, or the Latin, according to the words it may suit us to select as examples." [64]

But Hamilton is not interested in language for the sake of philology only; for him the study of language is a key to the history of the people who speak it:

"It is not solely in a philological view, that the study of languages is interesting. They afford the surest and most imperishable guide to the history of the nations who speak them, when their monuments are deficient. The

[63] *Ibid.*, p. 385.

[64] *Ibid.*, pp. 395-396.

Turks have long since lost their Tartar configuration: the flat faces and squat bodies of their ancestors are no longer remarked amongst their descendants, and have been succeeded by the fine forms which afforded models to Grecian artists. But their language remains an indelible monument of their origin; and whilst it continues to be spoken, will attest their descent from a tribe of Turcomans. The remains of Moorish magnificence in Spain will in time be obliterated; but the language of that country will, in all probability, never divest itself of the impression it received from the Arabian conquest." [65]

He once again shows here that his great admiration for William Jones's ideas does not prevent him from exercising his critical judgment:

"An attentive consideration of the language spoken by the civilized nations of the Old Continent, enabled Sir William Jones to trace the whole to three families, the Arabian, the Indian and the Tartar. Many he determined with certainty, and with perfect conviction to himself and to his readers. These, we will venture to predict, every future inquiry will only serve to confirm. Others were confessedly deduced from probable grounds and plausible conjectures: Their validity remains to be confirmed or disproved by subsequent researches; and that eminent scholar would have been the first to applaud this able attempt to illustrate the subject, however it may militate against his preconceived opinions." [66]

The review of the 10th volume of the *Asiatick Researches* was his last of that periodical. In the successive reviews devoted to volumes 6 to 10, Hamilton's enthusiasm already seemed to have been on the decline.

1811

Generally speaking, Hamilton seems to become discouraged. There may have been reasons of health we do not know of, but, whatever the reasons were, there obviously was a growing disenchantment. Hamilton appears to feel lonely, and to think that nobody in England really cares for Sanskrit studies and Indian culture. In our opinion, this attitude must be explained in the light of his stay in Paris. In Paris, he had lived in a circle of learned people many of whom were eager to learn everything about India and Sanskrit. When he came back to England, after the first satisfaction in being at home following his overlong detention in France, he missed the discussions he enjoyed in Paris. For the British India was much more a subject of political discussion than a subject of learning. There were, of course, many Englishmen who were interested in India and did research on that subject, but those were in Calcutta, not in London. In Paris, his status as a member of

[65] *Ibid.*, p. 390.
[66] *Ibid.*, pp. 390-391.

the Asiatic Society of Bengal had opened to him the most brilliant houses; in London, he was only one of many who had been in India and become interested in that country. There is no doubt that, in Hamilton's days, Sanskrit studies were almost restricted to the British, but it should be noted that these men were in India, while most of the people at home were not interested at all.

The review of Edward Moor's *Hindu Pantheon* in the 17th volume of the *Edinburgh Review*[67] affords the clearest evidence of Hamilton's loneliness:

"The work before us, we think, on the whole, an amusing one; and, if the subject were popular, might possibly become a popular one. That, however, is not likely soon to be the case. Our reasons for thinking so, are, like Mr Vellum's manifold. But, lest our readers should be in as great a hurry as the gentleman to whom he was speaking, we shall not give them quite so many as six. Some, however, they shall have. First, then, the few gentlemen qualified to throw light on the obscure subject of Hindu mythology, have not been pleased to communicate their ideas to the public; secondly, others, not so qualified, have been pleased to communicate theirs; thirdly, of the chosen few first mentioned, some have been pleased to publish extremely crude and hasty conjectures, and afterwards to retract them as hastily, with circumstances but little calculated to inspire confidence; lastly, and perhaps this reason might have sufficed, nobody here cares at all about the matter.

"Although it makes no figure in the minister's budget, the temporary suspension of pursuits purely literary, may be considered in the light of a war-tax, actually levied upon that portion of the community which can best afford to pay taxes. In the same manner, nearly, as a certain portion of the national capital is annually diverted from the channels into which it would otherwise have flowed, to supply the vacuum at the Exchequer, ('namque est in rebus inane'); so, a certain portion of floating intellect, usually expended in digging into antiquities, clearing away historical doubts, and sowing hypotheses, which seldom attain maturity, is now transferred to the consideration of the evanescent politics of the day. Without the operation of the sinking fund, expert calculators might determine, in what year, according to the present rate of progressive taxation, the national capital would be completely absorbed by the public debt; so, we presume, might it be predicted, with some approximation to accuracy, how long the war must last, in order to reduce our literature to political pamphlets and parliamentary reports.

"Situated as things are, indeed, we really consider a judicious limitation of an impertinent inquisitiveness about Hindu antiquities, and similar topics, as extremely salutary and reasonable. For, to bring the matter at once to a practical issue, Would an accurate translation of the Purānas, in the least

[67] No. 34, February 1811, art. 3, pp. 311-330. Attributed to Hamilton by *WIVP*.

curb the ambition of Buonaparte? What effect could the most profound commentary on the Veda have, in procuring for the nation a wise, a strong, and an energetic ministry? Would the price of candles be sensibly reduced, by the most luminous disquisition on the Hindu Triad? If the French intercept our teas and muslins and carry them into the Mauritius, will the ladies thank us for importing an old-fashioned assortment of antediluvian metaphysics? We protest, that all this appears to us perfectly conclusive. Nay, we cannot even conjecture what argument Brahmā himself could use at the Alien-office, to prevent his being ordered to quit the country, until six months after the conclusion of peace,—or at least until the resumption of cash payments by the Bank." [68]

Hamilton's authorship admits of no doubt. The following extract will suffice to prove it:

"We recollect, in particular, that the *Matsya Purāna* exhibits a very full code of laws for the guidance of the artist. . . The most copious treatise, however, on this subject that we have met with, is comprised in a work in the Imperial Library at Paris, entitled *Hayasiras*; but the manuscript did not specify from what purāna it was extracted. We subjoin an extract of it." [69]

The review of Moor's work, which contains extracts from the *Asiatick Researches*, gives Hamilton an opportunity to sum up his opinion about this periodical:

". . . a work of various merit, and unequal claims to confidence. Here we have the accuracy and erudition of Mr Colebrooke, mixed with the often fanciful, but always ingenious conjectures of Major Wilford; and the brilliant, but sometimes uncertain speculations of Sir William Jones." [70]

Essentially this review intends to offer some glimpses of Hamilton's ideas about one of his favorite subjects: comparative mythology. That these ideas are no longer held true is evident; but at least, his method is a sound one:

". . . our readers will remark, that our proofs do not rest, in this instance, on analogy of *sounds*, which may undoubtedly be fortuitous, but on that analogy, combined with the unity of the *attributes* denoted by those names, which it is impossible should be accidental." [71]

Hamilton totally accepts the opinion current in his time,

". . . that the mythology of all civilized nations of antiquity was susceptible of elucidation, from a collation with that of the Hindus." [72]

[68] *Ibid.*, pp. 311-312.
[69] *Ibid.*, p. 313.
[70] *Ibid.*, p. 314.
[71] *Ibid.*, p. 317.
[72] *Ibid.*, p. 323.

The 18th volume of the *Edinburgh Review* contains a review of Mark Wilks's *Historical Sketches of the South of India,*[73] which must be attributed to Hamilton. Besides Hamilton's favorite themes, we here find a reference to statements about the amount of land revenue made in his earlier review of Colebrooke's *Remarks on the Husbandry and Internal Commerce of Bengal,* which he now supports against Wilks's attacks. Moreover, he mentions a translation from Persian of an account of Haidar's life published in the *Asiatic Annual Register,* which had already been mentioned in the review of Stewart's *Descriptive Catalogue of the Oriental Library of the late Tippoo Sultan of Mysore,* and another similar translation of a description of Vijayanagar, which had been quoted in the review of Colebrooke's *Remarks,* two articles which we have examined above. Finally, the daybook of the East India Library attests that, on January 4, 1811, "2 Sets of Major Wilks's South of India" have been sent to Mr Hamilton.[74]

Once again Hamilton avails himself of the opportunity to express his conviction that the Hindus had a civilizing influence upon their Mohammedan conquerors:

"When, towards the close of the thirteenth century, Firoz the Second ascended the throne of Delhi, the northern provinces were already accustomed to the Mohamedan yoke. The milder manners and more civilized habits of the conquered people had begun to tame the ferocity of their conquerors; whilst their superior qualifications for business rendered their assistance indispensable, and assured them that degree of ascendancy which they have accordingly retained under every change of masters. But the immense measures, the magnificent structures, and the exuberant population, which had struck with astonishment the first invaders, had now disappeared. Rapine, fanaticism and the sword, had executed their task."[75]

He contends that the Hindu states prior to the Mohammedan rule were flourishing:

"For our own part, we are certainly inclined to hold, that the genius of the Hindu institutions, civil and religious, was calculated to produce a mild and patriarchal simplicity of government and manners, highly conducive to the prosperity of its subjects; whilst the Mohamedan rule has only been beneficial, when, receding from the genius of their own institutions, the Sultans have adopted or connived at the permanent regularity, the hereditary succession, and that attention to the promotion of agriculture, and the convenience of travellers, observed in the practice, and prescribed by the laws of the conquered

[73] No. 36, August 1811, art. 4, pp. 343-370. No attribution in *WIVP*.
[74] *Library Day Book 1801-1814.*
[75] In: *Ed. Rev.*, vol. 18, p. 344.

people. We fear, however, that we shall not obtain the sanction of Colonel Wilks to the truth of a conclusion, which, in our opinion, rests on the concurrence of Mohamedan writers, in representing each portion of Hindustan, successively subdued, in a state of higher prosperity, affluence and population, than it had afterwards obtained." [76]

As far as the description of the South of India is concerned, Hamilton gives extracts from the Purāṇas relative to that region. Starting from the word Deccan, he also engages in an etymological note about the cardinal points, which he introduces thus:

"The word *Decan,* in Sanscrit *Dex-in,* signifies south. For the amusement of the philologer, we insert a few remarkable analogies between the languages of the east and west, which it suggests." [77]

As to the rights of the zamīndārs, he comes back with new arguments to support the thesis he had enounced in his review of Colebrooke's *Remarks.*

1814

After the review of Wilks's *Historical Sketches* three volumes of the *Edinburgh Review* appear without an article by Hamilton. He resumes his contributions in the 22nd volume, with a review of J. Taylor's *Prabodh Chandrodaya, or the Rise of the Moon of Intellect, an Allegorical Drama; and Atma Bodh, or the Knowledge of Spirit; Translated from the Sanscrit and Pracrit.*[78] And this article bears new signs of his disenchantment caused by the lack of interest manifested for Indian antiquities:

"The Allegorical Drama for which we have now to claim the attention of our readers, is the greatest literary curiosity which, since the publication of Sacontālā, the learned research of our countrymen in the East, has presented to an ungrateful world." [79]

There can be no doubt that Hamilton is the reviewer, since he says:

"Our account of it has been delayed by a wish to compare it with the original Sanscrit: and having at length been so fortunate as to procure a copy from the East India Company's library, we have carefully collated them, and must pronounce Dr Taylor's translation to be as accurate, as the original is curious." [80]

In this review, Hamilton again complains that the system of transliteration proposed by William Jones has not been observed; he contends that Hinduism

[76] *Ibid.*, p. 355.
[77] *Ibid.*, p. 345, n.
[78] No. 44, January 1814, art. 8, pp. 400-409. Attributed to Hamilton by *WIVP*.
[79] *Ibid.*, p. 402.
[80] *Ibid.*, p. 402.

is more ancient than Buddhism: so many favorite themes of his. He also is of the opinion that Prakrit, far from being the language which served as a basis for the constitution of the refined language, is but a later corruption of Sanskrit.

The 23rd volume of the *Edinburgh Review* includes a review of two books by Wm. Marsden: *A Dictionary of the Malayan Language,* and *A Grammar of the Malayan Language,*[81] in which the author refers to the review of Leyden's article in the 10th volume of the *Asiatick Researches* in the following terms:

"We shall beg leave to quote an opinion which we offered on this subject, in our review of Dr Leyden's essay on the literature of Hindu-Chinese nations.

The words in which our sentiments were delivered, were as follow: . . ."[82] Since the review of Leyden's article was written by Hamilton, as we have seen above, it would be logical to infer that the present review of Marsden's books too, is due to Hamilton. The very text of this review however militates against such a conclusion. The author of this article has been lately in Malaysia, Indonesia, Indochina and China; he shows a personal knowledge of Javanese and Malay, of which he gives specimens. On the other hand, he does not seem to know much about India and Sanskrit. Several points on which he could easily have made comparisons with India—and where Hamilton would certainly not have neglected to do so—are not commented upon. Moreover, whereas the former reviews by Hamilton—including the one of Leyden's article— mention "Buddha," the present reviewer less technically speaks of "Budh."

On account of this conclusion, one might, of course, be tempted to deny Hamilton's authorship of the review of Leyden's article as well. Besides the grounds on which we attributed to him the review of the 10th volume of the *Asiatick Researches* as enumerated above, we must however mention that the review of Leyden's article shows, on the part of the author, a thorough knowledge of Sanskrit and no acquaintance at all with Malay and Javanese. The reference to the review of Leyden's article must have been made with respect to the *Edinburgh Review* generally and not the particular reviewer.

1815

In the 25th volume of the *Edinburgh Review* there is a review of Walter Hamilton's work: *The East India Gazetteer.*[83] Although there is no direct

[81] No. 45, April 1814, art. 7, pp. 151-189. *WIVP* hesitates between Hamilton and John Crawfurd.

[82] *Ibid.*, p. 172.

[83] No. 49, June 1815, art. 9, pp. 220-226. *WIVP* has no evidence to identify the author, but mentions Hamilton as a possibility.

reference to any former review, the text of the article itself indicates Alexander Hamilton as the author. Besides approval of Cornwallis's measures in Bengal —a position which becomes more and more isolated—, there is mention of the cities spoken of in the Purāṇas, and the situation of Hastināpura on the Ganges, points on which Hamilton has already insisted in the past. It is also but natural that Hamilton should wish to present to the public a work of his brother. Nothing, however, hints that author and reviewer are brothers.

The actual review of Walter Hamilton's work occupies only very little place. Alexander Hamilton rather seizes the new opportunity to defend Cornwallis's settlement of revenues in Bengal against the more and more frequent attacks it had to endure. To give new proofs that the rights which Cornwallis recognized to the zamīndārs were genuine, he goes to the extent of translating from Persian a deed which the zamīndār had to sign, under the Moghul empire, when he took possession of his estate. Hamilton even expects to come back to this point in the near future:

"In another article, we may probably consider the causes, which have hitherto operated to prevent the introduction of their permanent settlement, through the whole of the territories subject to Great Britain in India. It will probably appear that while procrastination was proper, expedient, and even necessary in some cases, that, in others, too much weight has been allowed to obstacles of a nature easily surmountable." [84]

This is not found, however, in any subsequent issues of the *Edinburgh Review.*

1816

The 26th volume of the *Edinburgh Review* contains a review of John Malcolm's *History of Persia, from the most early Period to the Present Time,*[85] which undoubtedly comes from Hamilton's pen, for there are references to his earlier reviews of Anquetil-Duperron's *Oupnekhat* and of Moor's *Hindu Pantheon.*

Hamilton once again shows great knowledge of the Greek and Latin geographers, and takes much interest in the identification of ancient and modern kings of Persia. As far as language is concerned, he believes that it has been exported from India to Persia:

"The origin and remote affinities of nations are soon lost in obscurity. Yet, of all historical monuments, the least disputable, and most enduring, is its language. The modern language of Persia is the offspring of the antient Pehlavi, itself a descendant of the still more venerable Zend. We consider this language as having existed, in its present form, only since the Arabian

[84] *Ibid.*, p. 226.
[85] No. 52, June 1816, art. 2, pp. 282-304. Attributed to Hamilton by *WIVP.*

conquest, and the Pehlavi to have prevailed from the time of Arbaces the Mede, who threw off the Assyrian domination. The writers who have treated of the intermediate period, always consider the Zend as a sacred language, confined to religious ceremonies, and of the highest antiquity. For the slender means we possess of judging of the Zend and Pehlavi, we are solely indebted to M. Anquetil du Perron.[86] The result of an examination will demonstrate, that the languages of Persia and India were, at one period, the same, or kindred dialects of an original tongue; and the resemblance is the most striking in the most antient specimens. Yet it is sufficient to turn up a modern Persic dictionary, in order to discover, that innumerable words are regularly derived from Sanscrit roots of similar import; or a modern grammar, to trace the same inflexions buried in the more complex structure of the Sanscrit. Many Persian words, names and titles, preserved by Greek writers, and which are destitute of meaning in modern Persic, present a distinct and appropriate sense in the cognate language. The fact, indeed, is little calculated to excite surprise, as the two countries are contiguous. Had the antient records of Persia been transmitted to an enlightened age; or did the traditions which survive, without replacing them, merit the name of history, we might expect to see unfolded the nature of that connexion which spread the language of the Brahmans from the shores of the Brahmaputra to the banks of the Tigris; and to ascertain whether it was unaccompanied with any of the remarkable institutions, which have, in all ages, distinguished the sons of Brahma." [87]

With the review of Malcolm's *History of Persia,* the long series of regular contributions which Hamilton made to the *Edinburgh Review* came to a close. He wrote one more article in the *Edinburgh Review* later on, but, as we shall see, this did not constitute a regular contribution; it was written with the sole purpose of helping the young Sanskritist Franz Bopp.

The reason why Hamilton ceased his regular contributions to the *Edinburgh Review* at this moment is not clear. Perhaps his health was deteriorating; perhaps his belief in the possibility of interesting his countrymen in Indian antiquities had totally disappeared. At any rate it should not be assumed that he actually broke with the editors of the *Edinburgh Review,* since, a few years later, he gave an isolated review of Bopp's works. Moreover, in the 27th volume of the *Edinburgh Review,* an article speaks highly of Hamilton, with respect to his teaching at the East India College. In a review of T. R. Malthus's *Statements respecting the East India College,* the author of the article joins with Malthus in defending the East India College from the charges brought against it; in this context he says: "It is not perhaps too much to suppose, that if the East India Company did not honour the instruc-

[86] Hamilton now obviously recognizes the value of Anquetil-Duperron's work, and does no longer consider as spurious the texts he published.

[87] *Ibid.,* pp. 282-283.

tors of their youth, by forming them into a Collegiate establishment, the talents of a Malthus and a Hamilton might have been withheld from the education of their servants." [88]

ELECTION TO THE ROYAL SOCIETY

In 1807 Hamilton was presented as a candidate for admission to the Royal Society. The certificate of his election has been preserved in the archives of the Royal Society:

"Alexander Hamilton Esq., Professor of Oriental languages in the East India Company's College at Hertford, a gentleman well skilled in several branches of Literature, being desirous of becoming a Fellow of the Royal Society; We whose names are hereunto subscribed do of our personal knowledge recommend him as being worthy of the honor he solicits and likely to become an useful and valuable member./ Read 28th May 1807 / 1st June 4 / 2—11 / 3—18 / 4 Nov: 5 / 5—12 / 6—19 / 7—26 / 8 Dec. 10 / 9—17 / 10—24 / Ballotted for & Elected 14th January 1808." [89]

The signatures subscribed are those of Benjamin Hobhouse, William Marsden, Charles Wilkins, John Walker, Thomas Murdoch, Matthew Raper, Charles Hatchett, Everard Home, William George Maton, Charles Francis Greville, Archibald Blair, and Henry Brougham.

Among the names of those who supported Hamilton's candidature, we notice, besides Henry Brougham, another Young Edinburgh Whig, Charles Wilkins, and his intimate friend and son-in-law William Marsden, the two most famous orientalists living in England at the time. Moreover, it should be noticed that they were the very first to sign the proposal, from which fact we may probably infer that the initiative was theirs. Once more, we thus see Hamilton appearing in very close connection with Charles Wilkins, and supported by him.

FRANK AND THE ELECTION TO THE MUNICH ACADEMY

Hamilton also had the privilege to be elected in 1815, together with Charles Wilkins, and with his colleague at Haileybury Charles Stewart, as a foreign member of the Munich Academy. This was meant as a token of gratitude for the help given to Othmar Frank.

Frank had obtained a grant from the Bavarian government to study Sanskrit in Paris first, in 1813, and in London thereafter, in 1814. His rival—as far as obtaining government funds was concerned—, Franz Bopp, came to London several years later. Hamilton helped both of these German scholars.

In his Sanskrit Grammar—the first one to be published in Germany—

[88] December 1816, pp. 516-517.

[89] The copyright of this document is the property of the Royal Society.

Frank recalls the Sanskrit lessons he enjoyed with Hamilton: "Quantum autem virorum clarissimorum *Colebrokii* et *Wilkinsii* operibus debeam, ac subsidiis, quantum primis cl. *A. Hamiltonii* institutionibus, grato animo agnoscere numquam desinam." [90] This sentence clearly expresses the situation prevailing for foreign Sanskrit scholars in London at the time. They could always count on the sympathy of the great orientalists Wilkins and Colebrooke; but in spite of the latters' readiness to help, their prominence permanently kept them at a distance. The man to whom the young men eager to learn Sanskrit turned when they needed constant practical support was Hamilton. Exactly the same relationship appeared làter with reference to Bopp.

Frank in his turn proposed to the Bavarian Academy the election of the Oriental scholars who had helped him in his studies. The history of the Academy which has recently been published on the occasion of its 200 years of existence relates the facts in the following terms: "Frank machte der Akademie den Vorschlag, Charles Wilkins, Alexander Hamilton und Charles Stewart zu korrespondierenden Mitgliedern zu wählen, dem bereitwillig statt gegeben wurde. Schelling brachte zum Ausdruck, dass solche Ehrung schon die Dankbarkeit fordere, 'welche ihnen die gelehrte Welt für ihre Bemühungen um die Indische und übrige morgenländische Literaturen, u. die Akademie insbesondere wegen der dem Prof. Frank geschenkten Unterstützung schuldig ist.'" [91] The election took place: "Hamilton, Stewart und Wilkins wurden 1815 in die Akademie aufgenommen, Colebrooke, gleichfalls auf Anregung O. Franks, im folgenden Jahre 1816, lauter Wahlen, die der Körperschaft zu hoher Ehre gereichen mussten." [92]

Prof. Dr. F. Bäthgen, the editor of this history of the Munich Academy, to whom we wrote for more detailed information, was kind enough to give us the following particulars: "Alexander Hamilton wurde nach einer im Akademiearchiv (Wahlakt 1815) vorliegenden 'Candidatenliste der zu auswärtigen ord. Mitgliedern der philosophischen Classe Vorgeschlagenen 1. Nov. 1815,' die nicht unterschrieben ist, der Handschrift nach von dem damaligen Sekretär der Philol.-philos. Kl. A. H. Fr. v. Schlichtegroll stammt, wahrscheinlich im November von der Ph.-ph. Kl. und danach in der allgemeinen Sitzung der AdW am 8.12.1815 (mit 14 weissen gegen 3 schwarze Kugeln) (Protokoll ds. Sitzg. im Protokollband d. allg. Sitzg. 1807-1816) zum ausw. ord. Mitgliede gewählt. Das Ministerium des Innern bestätigte die Wahl am 18.12.1815. In der zitierten 'Candidatenliste' wird Al. Hamilton als Professor für Hindu-Literatur und Geschichte Asiens 'in the East-India Company College at Haileybury' bezeichnet. Daneben steht folgender Randvermerk: 'Hamilton hat über die Pariser Sannscrit Ma(nu)sc(ri)pte einen Katalog verfertigt, den

[90] *Grammatica Sanscrita nunc primum in Germania*, Wirceburgi, 1823, p. XV.

[91] Baethgen: *Geist und Gestalt*, vol. I, pp. 92-93.

[92] *Ibid.*, vol. I, p. 101, n.

er mit Langles herausgab, einen ganz neuen Abdruck des Sannscrittextes des Hitopadesa besorgt.' Mehr konnte im Akademiearchiv über Al. Hamilton nicht festgestellt werden, da die vorhandenen Protokolle der Philol-philos. Kl. erst mit 1818 beginnen und einschlägige Korrespondenzakten nicht erhalten sind. An Sitzungen der BAdW dürfte Hamilton nie teilgenommen haben. Die Veröffentlichungen der BAdW in d. J. 1815-24 enthalten keine Studien von Hamilton und auch keinen Nekrolog auf ihn (Hilsenbeck, Register . . . 1807-1913)."

JOURNEY ON THE CONTINENT

During the summer of 1817, one year before he retired from Haileybury, Hamilton went on a journey to the Continent. He spent four weeks in Paris, where he undoubtedly visited his old friends Langlès and Chézy, and also went on to Germany. It is to be regretted that we know so little about this journey, and that we have no allusion to it at all by French scholars. In a letter written from Frankfurt on July 15, 1817, a passage of which has been quoted above, Friedrich Schlegel writes to his brother who was then residing in Paris: "Ungleich schlechter sind die (=news about Mme de Staël's health), welche ich von Alexander Hamilton, meinem alten Sanskrit-Freund vernahm, der dieser Tage hier durchkam; freylich waren seine Nachrichten nur vom Hörensagen, er hat eben wegen dessen, was er darüber gehört, gar nicht geglaubt, Deine Bekanntschaft machen zu konnen, was er sonst sehr gewünscht hätte, obschon er an 4 Wochen in Paris war; doch das wirst Du wohl von Bopp gehört haben, den er öfter sah und mit dem er sehr zufrieden war. Er war übrigens sehr freundschaftlich und ganz der alte treue Engländer oder Indianer." [93]

This was the first time that Hamilton met Bopp, as is confirmed by Bopp himself in a letter written from Paris on September 25, 1817, to his former teacher Windischmann: "Ich habe vor einigen Monaten Hamilton (und andere Orientalisten), der lange in Indien gewesen hier kennen gelernt." [94] One year later Bopp left for London, where he was to have frequent contacts with Hamilton.

[93] WALZEL: *op. cit.*, p. 568.
[94] LEFMANN: *op. cit.*, Anhang, p. 48.

CHAPTER VII

THE LAST YEARS

BOPP

In midsummer 1818 Hamilton retired from the East India College. It is not known where he lived after that time, but, since, even during his Professorship at Haileybury, he had an apartment in London, we may very well surmise that he went to live there. We are the more inclined towards such a supposition, because he now had contacts with German scholars such as Bopp and Lassen, and this most certainly occurred in London itself.

In October 1818 Franz Bopp left Paris for London, where he set to work immediately to have his *Nalus* printed. The model which was followed when printing this volume was Hamilton's edition of the Hitopadeśa. As early as December 16, 1818, the daybook of the Library of the East India Company reports: "Sent to Messrs Cox & Baylis (exemplar for Mr De Boppe [*corrected later to* Bopp] printing Sanskrita book) / 1 by Hitopadesa S. Liby Ed.," and again, on February 20, 1819: "Sent to Mr Cox for arranging page of M. Bopp's Nala & Damayanti / Hitopadesa. Sanskrit. Liby Edition."[1] Cox and Baylis thus became the publishers of the first Sanskrit book edited in Europe, Hamilton's *Hitopadeśa,* and of the second, Bopp's *Nalus,* both with Wilkins's characters. Bopp was aware of the fact, since he spoke of his 1819 edition of *Nalus* as "das zweite in Europa in alt-indischer Sprache gedruckte."[2]

Hamilton, who had met Bopp in Paris during the summer of 1817, had appreciated the young scholar, according to Schlegel's letter quoted above, and had recommended him to Colebrooke, and most probably also to Wilkins. In his first letter written from London to his former teacher Windischmann, Bopp says: "Auch sind hier Privatleute keine Freunde von Ausleihen ihrer Bücher. Glücklicher Weise macht Colbrooke hiergegen eine Ausnahme und ganz gegen meine Erwartung hat er mir bei meinem ersten Besuche erlaubt, ein Manuskript bey ihm abholen zu lassen. Auch gab er mir zu verstehen, dass er mir, wann mein Werk vollendet, welches ich jetzt drucken lasse und wovon ihm Hamilton, wie auch von meinem Conj. Syst. vortheilhaft geschrieben,— auch mit seiner kostbaren Sammlung über die Veda's aushelfen und mir gerne mit Rath und That beystehen werde."[3]

Bopp already knew Sanskrit too well to require lessons from Hamilton,

[1] *Library Day Book 1814-1820.*

[2] *Nalas und Damajanti. Eine Indische Dichtung aus dem Sanskrit übersetzt,* Berlin, 1838, p. VI.

[3] LEFMANN: *op. cit.,* Anhang, p. 58. The letter is dated March 1, 1819.

but it seems that the retired professor of Sanskrit took under his protection the young scholar, who again and again needed support to obtain the necessary grants from the Bavarian government. In a second letter written from London to Windischmann, at a moment when his *Nalus* had just been published, Bopp again refers to Hamilton's help: "Von den Orientalisten ist mein Werk mit sehr erfreulichem Beyfall aufgenommen worden; Hamilton, welcher auswärtiges Mitglied der Akademie zu München ist, hat darüber überaus vortheilhaft an dieselbe berichtet; Wilkins hat es der Ostind. Comp. bestens empfohlen und gerathen, sie solle 50 oder 100 Exemplare nehmen, letztens, wenn man auf der Orientalischen Schule davon Gebrauch machen wollte; dieses wünschte Professor Hamilton besonders, der mein Werk für die Schule sehr passend findet. Bey diesen Aussichten durfte ich also auf einen bedeutenden Absatz rechnen und erwarten meine Kosten gedeckt zu bekommen, allein gegen alle Vermuthung habe ich heute erfahren, dass die Comp. 6 Exemplare nehmen wolle, um sie nach Hertford zu schicken; Wilkins war darüber sehr befremdet und will nochmals für die Sache reden."[4]

We also learn that Hamilton mentioned Bopp's work to Chézy. From the letter written by Chézy to Bopp on September 18, 1819, it is however difficult to be sure whether Hamilton did so in a letter, or whether he made another journey to Paris during the summer 1819: "Mon cher Monsieur Bopp, j'ai reçu avec bien du plaisir votre savant ouvrage que j'ai lu avec beaucoup d'attention. Déjà Mr. Hamilton m'en avoit parlé, mais je ne croyois pas que vous y eussiez ajouté le texte ce qui lui donne un prix infini d'autant plus que vous y avez apporté un soin d'une correction bien extraordinaire."[5]

Hamilton also helped Bopp in another way: he lent him a manuscript of the Mahābhārata which he had in his possession. This manuscript was used by Bopp for his edition of *Nalus* referred to above. In the preface, Bopp duly acknowledges his debt while enumerating the manuscripts used for the edition: he collated his copy of a Parisian manuscript with a manuscript of the East India Library and two others belonging to the Jones collection, but he states: "Praecipue autem in emendato textu edendo summa nos adjuvit humanitas doctissimorum virorum H. T. Colebrooke et Alex. Hamilton, quorum codicem pulchre scriptum, cum Nìlacanthi scholiis, uterque nobis commendavit."[6] It should be remembered that even Colebrooke's manuscript was obtained with Hamilton's help, as appears from Bopp's letter to Windischmann quoted above.

In fact, Hamilton's manuscript was of much more use than Colebrooke's. On August 25, 1819, Bopp announced to Windischmann that Colebrooke had given his whole collection of manuscripts to the East India Library:

[4] *Ibid.*, Anhang, p. 59. The letter is dated August 25, 1819.

[5] *Ibid.*, Anhang, p. 127.

[6] *Nalus, Carmen Sanscritum e Mahàbhàrato*, London etc., 1819, pp. X-XI.

"Colebrooke hat seine ganze Bibliothek der Ostind. Comp. geschenkt, von ihm haben wir also nichts mehr zu erwarten."[7] This must be the reason why, in the preface to an edition of other episodes of the Mahābhārata, Bopp explicitly mentions the fact that the only manuscript which he could consult at home during his whole stay in London was Hamilton's: "Meine Pariser Abschrift verglich ich in London mit drei Dewanâgari-, sämmtlich mit Nîlakantha's Scholien versehenen, Handschriften. Hierbei kam mir besonders die freundschaftliche Güte des durch gründliche Kenntniss mehrerer Orientalischen Sprachen ausgezeichneten Hr. Alexander Hamilton zu statten, welcher mir die nöthigen Bände einer vollständigen Handschrift des Mahâ-Bhârata mittheilte, während ich die anderen nur auf der Ostindischen Bibliothek, mit welcher, während meines Aufenthaltes in London, auch Colebrooke's reichhaltige Sammlung einverleibt wurde, benutzen konnte. Die Hamiltonische Handschrift habe ich vollständig verglichen, die übrigen zog ich zu Rath wo es mir nothwendig schien."[8] Bopp even proposed to Burnouf senior to communicate to Burnouf junior the variant readings of Hamilton's manuscript for some other Mahābhārata episodes: "je vous communiquerai fort volontiers les variantes du manuscrit de Mr. Hamilton, ainsi que les explications du commentateur, que j'ai transcrites à Londres."[9]

It is again owing to Bopp, that we know what happened to Hamilton's manuscript after his death. In the preface to his second edition of the *Nalus*, Bopp enumerates all manuscripts used, and among them figures manuscript "*H.*, quem primo Alex. Hamiltonus, deinde hodiernus ejus possessor Gr. Ch. Haughtonius benevole mihi concesserunt."[10] Haughton, who held the Sanskrit chair in Haileybury after Hamilton's retirement, thus also became the possessor of the Mahābhārata manuscript after his predecessor's death.

LAST CONTRIBUTION TO THE *EDINBURGH REVIEW*

In 1819, Bopp was young and poor. He was in need of two things: reputation to obtain a professorship in Germany, and money to continue his studies and provide for the expenses of his publications. The best way to help him in both directions was to praise his books publicly. This must have been the reason why, after a long interruption, Hamilton sent a new contribution—his very last—to the *Edinburgh Review*. It consists of a review of two works of Bopp: the *Conjugationssystem der Sanskritsprache*, and the recently published *Nalus*. The review appeared in volume 33 of the *Edinburgh Review*, in

[7] LEFMANN: *op. cit.*, Anhang, p. 61.

[8] *Ardschuna's Reise zu Indra's Himmel, nebst anderen Episoden des Maha-Bharata*, Berlin, 1824, p. XXVI.

[9] LEFMANN: *op. cit.*, Anhang, p. 147.

[10] *Nalus Maha-Bharati Episodium*, altera emendata editio, Berlin, 1832, p. X.

May 1820.[11] There can be no doubt about the authorship of this article, since the author states that he also reviewed Wilkins's Sanskrit Grammar.

As Hamilton had already written to the Munich Academy in favor of Bopp's *Nalus*, in this article too, he obviously seems to address his encomium to the attention of a German public:

"The philologers of Germany, whose labours have so largely contributed to restore the text, explain the allusions, and elucidate the philosophy, of the writers of antient Europe, have at last begun to direct their attention to those of India. Mr Frederick Schlegel was the first, who, in an Essay on the language and philosophy of the Indians, indicated to his countrymen the sources of unexplored truths concealed in that distant region, and the important discoveries to which they might probably lead, in tracing the affiliation of nations, the progress of science, and the transactions of that mysterious period which precedes all history, but that of one remarkable family. Mr Schlegel's Essay, composed with that ability which has procured both for him and his brother a high rank amongst the literati of the Continent, excited the attention of the studious, and the patronage of the great. The former began to study Sanscrit through the medium of the slender resources furnished by the English press: And amongst the latter, the King of Bavaria sent two of his subjects, to seek, in Paris and in London, the necessary aid of Indian manuscripts. The two works before us prove the discernment which selected their author, as well as the liberal thirst of knowledge which prompted that monarch to encourage a pursuit, which even commercial jealousy herself could not attribute to a political motive, in a sovereign whose States are situated like those of Bavaria."[12]

Hamilton is conscious of the long interruption in his contributions to the *Edinburgh Review*, and gives a reason for not having reviewed Bopp's *Conjugationssystem* earlier; he reiterates his fear that his own field of interest is quite different from that of the general public:

"We should sooner have called the attention of our readers to the curious and instructive publication which stands at the head of this article, had we not despaired of rendering a grammatical disquisition interesting to the general reader. Some of our readers may possibly wish that we had persevered in that commendable diffidence."[13]

Hamilton apparently had the feeling that this was the last time he would write for the *Edinburgh Review*; the final pages of his article constitute nothing less than an authentic scientific testament:

[11] No. 66, art. 7, pp. 431-442. Attributed to Hamilton by *WIVP*.
[12] *Ibid.*, pp. 431-432.
[13] *Ibid.*, p. 432.

"The return of Mr Colebrooke to this country, who, after the death of Sir William Jones, contributed to the Asiatic Society the articles chiefly calculated to attract public attention, has rendered the publication of their researches less frequent, and their contents somewhat less interesting. We must, indeed, except some valuable additions to our geographical knowledge, from the observations of recent travellers, beyond the northern boundaries of Hindustan. The fields of Indian antiquities have been of late less diligently cultivated. As we may not again have an opportunity soon, we may be permitted here to cast a glance on those extensive regions.

"History, considered in a philosophical view, is chiefly conversant with the manners, opinions and circumstances, public and private, of individuals united in society. The manners of barbarians present everywhere a great similarity, modified only by climate. Of civilized nations, it may be affirmed, that the interest excited, and the inferences suggested, by their history, bear some proportion to the discrepancies it exhibits with the state of society which we habitually contemplate in our intercourse with the world. But these divergencies may very naturally be supposed to increase by remoteness of time. In our endeavours to rend the mysterious veil which ages have drawn between us and the nations of high antiquity, we are justified in expecting to trace moral combinations hitherto unremarked, political institutions unknown, and man acting under the influence of opinions and circumstances, to which we have not before seen him subjected.

"Although the succession of dynasties that have ruled, or of petty wars that have desolated particular countries, may not be entitled to much attention from the philosopher; yet the great revolutions which have dissolved antient societies, and produced new ones, sometimes sweeping from the earth all record of the preexisting order of things, must be known in order to account for what now exists. But these mighty events, with all their extensive train of moral consequences, have often occurred. England, though protected by the insular situation—*penitus toto diviso orbe Britannos,*—has at different periods witnessed the solemnities of the Druids, the holocausts to the Capitoline Jupiter, the barbarous rites of Woden and of Freya, and, finally, the establishment of the true faith.

"It is probable that none of these great landmarks have perished, since the age in which Homer lived, with respect to Greece, and since the reigns of Cyaxares and of Alyattes in Asia. But what would have been the astonishment of the Father of History, could he have been informed, that, of the language in which he spoke and wrote, the most cognate dialect was that of India,—a country so remote, that even his inquisitive mind had learned little respecting it, excepting that it was the most populous of countries then known?—That the divinities worshipped by his countrymen, which he generally states to have been recently introduced into Greece from Egypt, by Homer and succeeding poets, had their altars established on the shores of the distant

Ganges, where they were destined to continue for ages, after they had abandoned Olympus? The causes to which these unquestionable facts are to be attributed, are beyond the period of history;—but are they also lost to tradition?—Into the immensely voluminous literature of the Brahmans, who has sufficiently penetrated to answer this question?

"Independently of this curious problem, the civil history of India, from the era at which the Puranas professedly date, to the period of the Musulman invasion, is an object of rational inquiry; and its chronology might, to a certain extent, be supported by establishing synchronisms, such as identifying Chandra Gupta with Sandracottus. The name of the Indian sovereign who reigned over Magadha, when Behmen (Vahuman endowed with arms), whom the Greeks call Artaxerxes Longimanus, invaded the west of India, is preserved by a Persian historian, and accords with the Indian genealogies. Such synchronisms, when they can be discovered, afford confirmation to other facts.

"To the Geography of the Puranas, we earnestly wish that some of the members of the learned Society to which we have alluded, would devote their attention: but not merely by specifying the situation of countries incidentally mentioned in other works. Each Purana contains a chapter on geography, usually entitled 'Bhuvana darsa,' or the mirror of regions. A similar work seems to have been current in antient Persia, which M. Anquetil du Perron translated from the Pehlevi, with the title of Bhaun deesh. If a Sanscrit scholar in India, taking for his text one of those Puranica chapters, would give a local habitation and a modern name to the countries, he would supply an important desideratum; and might derive great aid from the Pandits, and from the strangers who now resort to Calcutta from all parts of India. The names of antient nations, of whom the Hindus have retained little besides, attest the authenticity of their traditions; as the Pehleva, the Sacae, and, more recently, the Huna. Ptolemy places in northern Asia, a region which he terms Ottorcora. The Uttara Curu, or northern land of the Curus, is allotted to the same quarter in the Purana.

"An inquiry of an extremely interesting nature might also be made into the doctrines of the different schools of Philosophy, with a view to ascertain whether the sects founded by Pythagoras, Epicurus, Zeno, Plato, and Aristotle, stand in the relation of parents or offspring, to the sects supporting similar opinions in the East.

"With respect to Science, we certainly never supposed that the discoveries of Newton or of La Place had been anticipated by the Brahmans: nor that the existing boundaries of scientific knowledge were likely to be extended by our intercourse with India. We still think, however, that the *history* of science may derive important contributions from that source. The discussions to which the publication of the Indian Algebra gave rise, have elicited some valuable information. Before we determine that the knowledge existing in the East, and bearing the marks of originality by the peculiarity of its forms, ought to be attributed to the Greeks, it should, we think, be very distinctly demonstrated, that the Greeks themselves possessed what they are said to have communicated."[14]

AN APOCRYPHA: *A KEY TO THE CHRONOLOGY OF THE HINDUS*

The British Museum Catalogue, followed by the *DNB* and the *DIB*, attributes to Hamilton a work published anonymously in 1820, the full title of which is: *A Key to the Chronology of the Hindus; in a Series of Letters, in which an Attempt is made to facilitate the Progress of Christianity in Hindostan, by proving that the Protracted Numbers of All Oriental Nations when reduced agree with the Dates given in the Hebrew Text of the Bible.*[15] We do not know the grounds upon which the British Museum cataloguer has attributed the volume to Hamilton. As a matter of fact, it should be noted that in the catalogue itself the title is followed merely by the notation "by A. H.," which is however not to be found in the work itself. Even if the catalogue is right as far as the initials A. H. are concerned, we cannot agree that this A. H. is Alexander Hamilton, at least not the Alexander Hamilton we are concerned with.

The author of *A Key to the Chronology of the Hindus* states that the letters, which constitute the two volumes, were written in 1815, and published in 1820 while he was absent from England—and this probably means that he was still in India at the time—: "an explanatory Glossary is affixed, which will in some degree rectify those typical errors, which occur in consequence of the unavoidable absence of the Author, when the Letters were in the press."[16]

His main purpose is to convert the Hindus to Christianity, and he acknowledges that he has worked in this direction for a long time. His very first letter begins with the following statements: "In compliance with your request, I have arranged the observations, which a long residence in India enabled me to make, on the Theology and Chronology of the Hindus: subjects little understood, but which every young man, who enters in the East India Company's service, should endeavour to become master of; more especially since the conversion of the Hindus to Christianity has become a consideration with the English government, and which may, I am confident, be effected with ease, if proper methodes are adopted. On this subject, I speak from personal knowledge, having devoted much time to so desirable an object: and had it not interfered with the mercenary views of an individual, the protestant religion had long since been introduced not only in the district of Dindigul, but in all the Polloms subordinate thereto. I shall be most happy, if my researches prove either beneficial or amusing to you. They may possibly

[14] *Ibid.*, pp. 440-442.

[15] 2 vol., Cambridge, Rivington, XX-402 and 415 pp.

[16] *Ibid.*, vol. I, p. IV.

prevent you from imbibing those prejudices which Europeans in general too readily adopt, and which have of late years been greatly strengthened, by the works of Mr. Bryant and Sir William Jones. From the latter you will gain much useful information, provided you guard against his System of Chronology, which is erroneous throughout."[17]

Apart from the harsh attack against William Jones, which contrasts sharply with Hamilton's admiration, we must bring to the fore that the author lives—or has lived—in Dindigul. Whereas Hamilton has lived in Calcutta, the author of the *Key* appears to have lived in Dindigul and mentions monuments of the South of India only, as, for instance, in the following passages: "In the little district of Dindigul, I ascertained that there were more than ten thousand, who believed in the Incarnation of Christ";[18] "There are several pagodas, or temples, sacred to this worship, in one of which the symbol of the Deity is a man with three heads: and at the great pagoda of Travancore, the symbol is a serpent with a thousand heads";[19] "First, every eastern nation believes that the more noble buildings of the antediluvian world were not destroyed, and many choultries and temples still extant, being excavations of the solid rock could neither be injured by time nor climate, and are just as likely to have been the works of artists of the old world, as of those of the early ages of the new world. Of these Mavaliporam may be considered one";[20] "His (=Kṛṣṇa's) history, according to the Brahmans, is still to be seen engraved in sculpture, in one of the caves of Mavaliporam of unfathomable antiquity."[21]

Against Hamilton's caution when it comes to the establishment of synchronisms, which is still apparent in the review of Bopp's works cited above, the author of the *Key* extravagantly brings together Hindu, Chinese, Egyptian and Hebraïc chronologies. Whereas, following William Jones's example, Hamilton again and again drew comparisons between Hindu and Greek mythologies, the author of the *Key* tries to reduce Hinduism to a kind of monotheism, and insists on the *trimūrti* as corresponding to the trinity in Christianity. In short, the whole book is in flagrant contradiction to all Hamilton's well established opinions. It is perhaps not out of place also to quote the disparaging words about the book by Hamilton's friend Langlès: "je n'examinerai pas non plus à quel point sont fondées les assertions du savant et biblique auteur anonyme de la *Clef de la chronologie des Hindoux*."[22] After what has been said in previous chapters of the present volume we dare see in these words another indication that the *Key to the Chronology of the Hindus* should not be attributed to Hamilton.

[17] *Ibid.*, vol. I, pp. 1-2.
[18] *Ibid.*, vol. I, p. 2.
[19] *Ibid.*, vol. I, p. 9.
[20] *Ibid.*, vol. I, p. 385.
[21] *Ibid.*, vol. II, p. 211.
[22] *Monuments anciens et modernes de l'Hindoustan*, vol. I, p. 217.

THE ROYAL ASIATIC SOCIETY

Hamilton lived long enough to witness the foundation of the Royal Asiatic Society of Great Britain and Ireland, in March 1823, and he was among its very first members. The first volume of the *Journal of the Royal Asiatic Society of Great Britain and Ireland*, published in 1834, mentions Alexander Hamilton in the list of members deceased since the institution of the society.[23]

THE END

Although we know very little about Hamilton's last years, we are inclined to think that his health was gradually declining. In a letter to Johannes Schulze written on February 20, 1824, *i.e.* ten months before Hamilton's death, August Wilhelm Schlegel speaks of total retirement on the part of Hamilton: "Alexander Hamilton, der ehemals meinem Bruder in Paris manches mittheilte, nachher Professor in Hayleybury war, hat sich ganz von der gelehrten Welt zurückgezogen. Er war wohl überhaupt nicht sonderlich stark." [24]

Whether or not Hamilton regularly lived in Liverpool in 1824, we do not know. Anyhow, it was in that city that he died on December 30, 1824. The news was immediately known in London, since Christian Lassen, who lived in London at the time, announced Hamilton's death to his former teacher A. W. Schlegel in a letter dated January 3, 1825: "Alex[ander] Hamilton ist vor wenigen Tagen gestorben." [25]

We have already quoted in the introduction the obituaries which some British journals devoted to Hamilton, very brief notices indeed. The only worthy obituary that we know of was published in the *Journal Asiatique* in Paris; even after his death, Hamilton as a scholar must have been much more highly appreciated in France than in his own country:

"M. Alexandre Hamilton, l'un des savans qui se sont occupés avec le plus de succès et de la manière la plus utile de la langue samskrite, est mort à Liverpool, le 30 décembre 1824. Il était professeur de samskrit et de littérature indienne, au collége des langues orientales à Haileybury. Ce savant distingué est, comme on le sait, auteur du catalogue des manuscrits samskrits de la Bibliothèque royale de Paris. Ce catalogue fut composé d'abord en anglais en l'an 1807 [26] lors d'un voyage que M. Hamilton fit en France. Personne parmi nous ne connaissait alors la langue samskrite; M. Hamilton fut le premier qui contribua à mettre en ordre cette partie des manuscrits de la

[23] London, pp. LXII-LXIV.

[24] Josef Koerner (ed.): *Briefe von und an August Wilhelm Schlegel*, 2 vol., Zürich etc., [1930], vol. I, p. 410.

[25] Kirfel: *op. cit.*, p. 105.

[26] This is an error. Hamilton had left Paris in 1806 after having compiled the catalogue. 1807 is the year in which the French translation was published.

Bibliothèque Royale. Son catalogue fut bientôt après traduit et publié en français par M. Langlès, qui le grossit de quelques notes extraites des Mélanges Asiatiques de Dalrymple et des Mémoires de la Société de Calcutta. Cette traduction parut successivement dans le Magasin Encyclopédique de l'année 1807; un certain nombre d'exemplaires furent tirés à part, de manière à former un petit volume de 118 pages in-8°, Paris, 1807. M. Hamilton a encore publié dans quelques recueils anglais des articles relatifs à l'ancienne géographie de l'Inde; ils sont curieux et fort savans, et dignes d'être plus connus. Nous nous proposons de les reproduire dans ce journal, et nous croyons qu'ils seront bien accueillis des savans qui s'intéressent aux progrès des connaissances qui ont l'Inde pour objet. Il est assez extraordinaire qu'aucun journal anglais n'ait consacré un article nécrologique un peu étendu à la mémoire de ce savant distingué." [27]

UNKNOWN ARTICLES ABOUT ANCIENT INDIAN GEOGRAPHY

The editors of the *Journal Asiatique* seem to have neglected the promise expressed in Hamilton's obituary: one vainly looks for French translations of Hamilton's articles in the following numbers. The *BU* and the *NBG* have been misled by the announced publication: both erroneously mention that Hamilton's articles about ancient Indian geography were actually translated in the *Journal Asiatique*.[28]

It is unfortunate that Hamilton's obituary in the *Journal Asiatique* does not specifically mention the names of the journals in which Hamilton published the said articles. In spite of all our efforts we have not been able to discover them. We, however, do believe that they exist—most probably anonymously published—: the geographical chapters in the Purāṇas were one of his favorite topics, as we have seen in several of Hamilton's contributions to the *Edinburgh Review*.

UNPUBLISHED SANSKRIT DICTIONARY

Adelung reports that Hamilton left a manuscript of a Sanskrit dictionary, which was offered for sale after his death: "'an Original Dictionary, Sanscrit and English, by *Alex. Hamilton.*' Befand sich handschriftlich im Besitze der Buchhändler Howell & Stewart in London. S. Oriental Catalogue for 1827, Suppl. p. 102." [29] It is most probable that Hamilton never intended to publish it, but that he gradually composed his dictionary in the course of his readings and for his own private use. It is not known whether the manuscript still exists, and, if so, where it is preserved.

[27] 7, October 1825, pp. 255-256.

[28] The *DNB* and the *DIB* mention magazine articles on ancient Indian geography, on information drawn from the *Journal Asiatique*

[29] *Bibliotheca Sanscrita,* p. 57.

CONCLUSION

We are fully aware of the dangers which lurk in the course of writing a biography. Constant contact with and growing interest in the object of one's researches might so easily lead to the creation of a false perspective, and to overestimating the part played by one's hero.

There is no reason to hide the fact that, as our work went along, the figure of Alexander Hamilton became more and more alive, and that, as we learned more details about his personality, we developed a certain affection towards the affable and good tempered man who seems to have been liked by everyone who came to know him personally.

It is equally true that we became more and more fascinated and impressed by Alexander Hamilton as a scholar, and by the important part he played in the development of Sanskrit studies in particular and Indic studies in general. Although the previous pages were written with the specific purpose to produce evidence of Hamilton's importance for the history of Indology in Europe, we are nevertheless convinced that we are not guilty of exaggerating his merits. On the contrary, we consider to have done justice—122 years after his death—to a pioneer who, for a number of reasons, has never received the attention he undoubtedly deserved.

One of the reasons why Hamilton remained practically unknown to the scholarly world is his habit of publishing his works anonymously. The enumeration of the books and articles which we attributed to him in this volume speaks for itself; and we are convinced that we have not been able to provide the reader with a complete survey of Hamilton's writings. Unfortunately, for a reason which it is difficult to ascertain, he preferred to leave both his articles and his books unsigned. Apart from the catalogue of the National Library in Paris, the name Alexander Hamilton does not appear in any of the writings on India. The various indirect kinds of evidence we had to appeal to in the above pages will be enough to show how difficult it is to trace Hamilton's contribution.

The main reason, however, why Hamilton never attracted any special attention, is that those who did come across his name were satisfied with the knowledge that he had been the one to initiate the great Friedrich Schlegel in Sanskrit. Hamilton's teaching Sanskrit in Paris generally and to Schlegel in particular is about the only fact which is repeated again and again—often not too correctly—in various volumes dealing with the early history of Sanskrit in Europe. Schlegel's influence upon the propagation of Sanskrit and Indic studies in the West may have been considerable and worthy of all our attention. It is to be remembered, however, that, as far as his knowledge of Sanskrit is concerned, he never attained any extraordinary heights, certainly not the heights reached by his Sanskrit teacher.

Far too often the impression has been created as if Hamilton's role was limited to merely initiating Schlegel into the ancient language of India. Even if it is not said in so many words, it is at least suggested that Hamilton was only an instrument, introducing into Schlegel's strong intellect a new element which only there became active and fruitful. To this impression we have to oppose the fact that Schlegel not only learned Sanskrit from Hamilton, but that his views were actually influenced by the latter.

The fact that Hamilton was thus able to influence the brilliant Friedrich Schlegel bears witness to an element which also is evident in many other ways: Hamilton's strong personality. Hamilton is not only important through the intermediary of his pupils; he in truth, is a giant, independent of anybody else. His knowledge of Sanskrit and of India generally was an extremely vast one. Such must already have been the opinion of Wilkins, who never failed to support his younger countryman. Moreover, the fact that he was capable of compiling a catalogue of the Sanskrit manuscripts in Paris, the fact also that in his writings he quotes from a large variety of Sanskrit texts, proves the great ease with which Hamilton read all kinds of Sanskrit literature. This accomplishment deserves to be stressed here once again; few are the Sanskritists outside India whose readings have been as extensive as those of Alexander Hamilton.

Notwithstanding all this, Hamilton's knowledge of Sanskrit has been severely criticized. No doubt, August Wilhelm Schlegel and Lassen were right when they pointed out a number of errors in the edition and analysis of the Hitopadeśa. First of all, progress in the knowledge of Sanskrit was so swift at the time that it was easy for a good Sanskrit scholar to find fault even with his immediate predecessors. But there was more: A. W. Schlegel and Lassen had come to Sanskrit via a thorough German training in classical philology; they were to conduct Sanskrit philology along the same lines, against the background of such concepts as critical editions and textual criticism. It would be wrong not to give them due credit for the important element they contributed to the study of Sanskrit in Europe.

To correctly assess Hamilton's role as compared to his—mainly—German successors it has to be borne in mind that his Anglo-Saxon background was completely different from the one represented by such men as A. W. Schlegel and Lassen. Moreover, his Sanskrit undoubtedly bore the impact of those who had been his teachers in India: the pandits. Even before we had found Horner's above quoted reference to "the pandit," Hamilton repeatedly reminded us of the typical approach of the Indian pandits of whom he must have been a worthy disciple. His uncommon fluency in all fields of Sanskrit literature, his enjoying studying and teaching the language rather than indulging in writing about it extensively, and—we are tempted to add—his attaching so little importance to having his name added to his writings, all this brings him so close to the bearers of knowledge in the country he had come to love.

Hamilton was, however, not important as a Sanskritist only. In view of the close relations which were soon to be established between Sanskrit and comparative Indo-European philology, a few words must be added about Hamilton's influence on the latter. Here again his name has been forgotten in favor of somebody who, without being his student, as was the case with Schlegel, derived much help from him; we mean: Franz Bopp. We all look upon Bopp's *Conjugationssystem* as the successful beginning of comparative philology; but we have forgotten that it was Hamilton who was called upon by the author, himself, to support his publication by means of an extensive and laudatory review.

Moreover, without implying that Hamilton played an active part in the elaboration of comparative philology as such, we came to the conclusion that an analysis of his ideas is extremely important to counteract a widespread but oversimplified conception. Too often modern authors create the impression that comparative Indo-European philology actually started with Bopp's *Conjugationssystem*. Numerous passages from Hamilton's writings quoted above show that, even before 1816, the ground for comparative studies was well prepared, and that Bopp's genius was more responsible for creating the scientific method than for conceiving the idea.

Hamilton's biography is far from complete. Notwithstanding all our efforts a number of points remained obscure, either because documents do not exist, or because we were not able to trace them. We nevertheless decided to present the result of our researches to the public. Perhaps the attention of a worker in a related field will thus be drawn to Alexander Hamilton and to documents about him which he himself came across in the course of his researches. We shall be grateful if any such research worker will in due time complete the present biography; or, if he is kind enough to communicate to us any new data, we shall be glad to examine them and perhaps, in future, publish additions to the present volume.

INDEX NOMINUM

[Numbers refer to pages; italics indicate names appearing in the notes only. To facilitate bibliographical references, names of modern authors are included.]

Addiscombe Seminar, *74*.
Adelung, Friedrich von, 39, 43, *79*, 121.
Alger, John Goldworth, *10*, 33, *39*.
Allen, John, 12, 81.
Anderson, 15.
Anquetil-Duperron, Abraham Hyacinthe, 16-17, 23-25, *40*, *43*, 56, 61, 83, 91, 107, 108, 117.
Anville, Jean Baptiste Bourguignon d', 84.
Arrowsmith, Aaron, 31.
Asiatic Annual Register, 13-30, 31-32, 81, 93, 104.
Asiatic Society, of Bengal, 6, 8, 18, 20, 35, 37, 42, 43, 51, *55*, 60, 62, 63, 86, 102, 116, 121.
Asiatick Researches, 6, 8, 20, 23, 25-30, 35, 39, 42, 43, 82-88, 89, 90-93, 95, 96, 98-101, 103, 106, 121.

Bäthgen, Friedrich, *3*, 110-111.
Baldwin, George, *22*.
Basham, Arthur Llewellyn, *2*, *6*, 63.
Bayer, Gottlieb Siegfried, 98.
Bayerische Akademie der Wissenschaften, *see* Munich Academy.
Benfey, Theodor, *2*, *3*.
Bentley, John, 25, 29-30, 90-91.
Bernstein, Georg Heinrich, 73, 76.
Bertram, Johann Baptist, *47*; *see also* Boisserée, Sulpiz.
Bibliothèque Impériale, Nationale, Royale de France, *see* National Library of France.
Black & Co., 74.
Blair, Archibald, 109.
Blunt, James T., 86.
Boisserée, Melchior, *47*; *see also* Boisserée, Sulpiz.
Boisserée, Sulpiz, 47-49.
Bopp, Franz, 52, 53, 57, 62, *63*, 76, 77, 79, 80, 108, 109, 111, 112-115, 119, 124; Biography and correspondence, *see also* Lefmann.
Bréal, Michel, 62-63.
British Museum, 18.
Brougham, Henry Peter, Lord, 12, 38, *98*, 109.
Brown, Thomas, 12.
Bryant, Jacob, 119.
Buchanan, Francis, 25-28, 93-94, 99.
Buckland, Charles Edward, *1*.
Bülow, Heinrich von, 76.
Burn, Richard, *2*, *18*.
Burnouf, Eugène, 62, 114.
Burnouf, Jean Louis, 61-62, 114.

Cadell, Thomas, & Davies, William, 31-32.
Campbell, Charles, 9.
Campbell, Lawrence Dundas, 14, 30, 31, 32, 81-82, 88.
Carey, William, 67, 78, 80, 100.
Chambers, Raymond Wilson, 2, *18*, 37, 52, *55*, 64, 95, 96.
Chambers, 15.
Charavay, Marie Etienne, 38.
Chatterjee, Atul, *2*, *18*.
Chézy, Antoine Léonard de, 45, 46, 47, 50-51, 53, 55, 56, 59-61, 62, 63, 84, 111, 113; Biography, *see also* Chezy, Helmine von; Sacy.
Chezy, Helmine von, *3*, 10, 36, 38, 45-49, 59, 60.
Cockburn, Henry, Lord, *3*, 8-9, 10, 11, 12, *34*, *35*, *81*.
Colebrooke, Henry Thomas, 39, *43*, 60, 82, 86, 88-90, 93, 94, 99, 100, 103, 104, 105, 110, 112, 113-114, 116.
Collège de France, 59, 61, 62.
College of Fort William, 6, 68.
Congreve, William, 74.
Copinger, Walter Arthur, 12, 22, 23, 82, 88, 89, 90, 93, 95, 98.
Cornwallis, Charles, Lord, 6-9, 19, 100, 107.
Cox, Henry C. M., *10*.
Cox, Hiram, 9-10.
Cox & Baylis, *73*, 79, 112.
Crawfurd, John, *106*.
Croydon Seminar, *see* Addiscombe.
Cuvier, Georges, baron, 86.

Dalrymple, Alexander, 121.
Danvers, Frederick Charles, 65-66.
Darmesteter, James, *2*.
Debrett, John, 31.
Dodwell, Edward, *5*.
Dussieux, Louis Etienne, 52, 61.
Du Theil, François Jean Gabriel de la Porte, 84.

East India College, 1, *40*, 64-80, 81, 98, 108-109, 110, 112, 113, 114, 120; History, *see also* Danvers; Monier-Williams.
East India Library, 19, 64, 67, 69, 73-74, 75, 79-80, 104, 105, 112, 113-114.
East India Press, 72-74, 75.
Ecole des Langues Orientales Vivantes, 63.
Edinburgh Review, 11-13, 14, 15, 22-30, 64, 81-109, 114-118, 121.
Ekenstoun, 75.
Elgin, Thomas Bruce, Lord, 33.
Ernst, Charlotte, *48*.

Fauriel, Claude, 53, 55-57, 58, 62, 63; Biography, *see also* Guigniaut; Ozanam; Sainte-Beuve.
Filliozat, Jean, *40*, *41*, *54*, 55, 61.
Forbes, James, 38.
Fouché, Joseph, duc d'Otrante, 36, 37-38, 55.
Fourmont, Etienne, 55.
Frank, Othmar, 109-110.

Galley, Jean Baptiste, 53, 56-57, *59*.
Garratt, Geoffrey Theodore, *2*.
Gaulmier, Jean, 37-38, 55.
Genlis, Stéphanie Félicité Brulart de, 49.
Gilchrist, John Borthwick, 65, 66.
Gildemeister, Johann, 80.
Gordon, 75.
Gossellin, Pascal François Joseph, 84.
Grant, Charles, 68.
Grellmann, Heinrich Moritz Gottlieb, 87.
Greville, Charles Francis, 109.
Guigniaut, Joseph Daniel, 53, 56, *59*.

Hagemann, Gottfried, 47-49, 50, 54, 62.
Haileybury College, *see* East India College.
Halhed, Nathaniel Brassey, 17, 83, 94.
Hamilton, George, 3.
Hamilton, Walter, 3-4, 32-33, 42, 106-107.
Hamilton, William Richard, 33.
Harington, John Herbert, 86.
Hastfer, Helmine von, *see* Chezy, Helmine von.
Hatchett, Charles, 109.
Haughton, Graves Chamney, 70-72, 77, 80, 114.
Heberle, J. M., *80*.
Henington, 75.
Hertford College, *see* East India College.
Heyne, Christian Gottlob, 51.
Hilsenbeck, Adolf, 111.
Hobhouse, Benjamin, 109.
Hodges, William, *43*.
Hodson, Vernon Charles Paget, *3*, *5*, 8, *66*.
Holbach, Paul Heinrich Dietrich, baron von, 49.
Holland, Saba, Lady, 95.
Holtei, Karl von, *47*.
Home, Everard, 109.
Horner, Francis, 22, 35, 68-69, 81, 123; Memoirs and correspondence, *see also* Horner, Leonard.
Horner, Leonard, *12*, *69*.
Howell & Stewart, 121.
Humboldt, Wilhelm, baron von, 76, 77.

Imperial Library of France, *see* National Library of France.
Impey, Elijah, 38.
Impey, Elijah Barwell, *38*.
Institut de France, 56, 86.

Jeffrey, Francis, Lord, 10, 11, 12, 22, 34, 35, 38, 68, 81, 89; Biography, *see also* Cockburn.
Johnson, Francis, 79.
Joinville, 87.
Jones, William, 5, 6, 17, 20, 22, 27, 35, 39, 41, 43, 56, 60, 62, 83, 85, 86, 91, 94, 95-96, 101, 103, 105, 113, 116, 119.
Journal Asiatique, 1, 120-121.

Keene, Henry George, 65.
Kirfel, Willibald, 77, *120*.
Klette, Anton, 57-58.
Körner, Josef, *47*, *48*, *50*, *51*, 57-58, *120*.

Labaume, A., *42*.
Langlès, Louis Mathieu, 3-4, 34, 35, 37, 39-44, 51, 55, 60, 62, 63, 74, 75, 76, 82-83, 95, 111, 119, 121.